STORM TACTICS
HANDBOOK

Storm Tactics Handbook

Modern Methods of Heaving-To
for Survival in Extreme
Conditions

By Lin and Larry Pardey

**PARDEY
BOOKS**

The text of this book is composed in Garamond and Helvetica
Produced by SAIL Magazine
Cover design by Rob Johnson
Editing and layout by Sarah Day
Production by Allison Peter
Manufactured by Thomson-Shore Inc.
Photograph of authors by Helen J. Meier

Library of Congress number 95-92144

ISBN 0-9646036-6-7

Published by Pardey Books

Distributed by Paradise Cay Publications
        P.O. Box 29
        Arcata, CA 95578-0029
        USA
        800-736-4509

Printed in the United States of America

Printing history
    First printing 1995
    Second printing 1996
    British printing 1996
    Third printing, updated edition 1997
    Second British printing 1999
Printed on recycled paper
    Fourth printing 2000

Heave-to, to lay a sailing ship on the wind with her helm a-lee and her sails shortened and so trimmed that as she comes up to the wind, she will fall off again on the same tack and thus make no headway. The whole idea in heaving-to is to bring the wind on to the weather bow and hold the ship in that position where she rides most safely and easily.

—*From the* Oxford Companion to Ships and the Sea, *Edited by Peter Kemp*

Each vessel varies in terms of the best method for heaving-to, and it is difficult to lay down hard and fast guidelines. Nevertheless, it is essential that before going offshore, yacht skippers are aware of the best way of heaving-to their particular vessel so that it lies better to the weather.

Sea anchors/drogues. Consideration should be given to amending the requirements of Category 1 survey to provide for appropriately sized drogues or sea anchors to be carried on yachts. At present there is no such provision.

—*From the report issued by the New Zealand Maritime Safety Authority after a thorough investigation of the loss of lives and yachts in the "Queen's Birthday" storm between Tonga and New Zealand in the first week of June 1994.*

Acknowledgments

A ssistance for this project came from many sources. It is difficult to include all of them, as some ideas were sparked by conversations we had, articles we read, stories we heard 20 or 25 years ago. But we would like to thank the following people for their input and encouragement.

Louis and Pat DeBeers, Klaus and Wilma Schade, who, along with Gordon's Bay Rescue Service crew, took their boats out with forecasts of 45 knots of wind to assist in testing heaving-to and para-anchor usage on fin-keeled cruisers.

Mara Blumer and Helio Viana, who arranged for us to use their air-conditioned apartment for final editing of this handbook.

Tom Linskey, Victor Shane, and the people named throughout this text who gave us permission to use their stories.

Patience Wales, editor of SAIL Magazine, for her encouragement, assistance, and suggestions, Sarah Day for her work as editor and organizer of this edition, and Rob Johnson for his work in designing the cover and working with us on photographs and layout.

Roger Taylor read and edited this manuscript. His suggestions have been incorporated here. Thanks also to Kathleen Narney for her help and enthusiasm.

George Taylor, editor of *Practical Boat Owner,* in England; Peter Bruce, editor of Adlard Coles, *Heavy Weather Sailing;* and Peter Blake, well-known New Zealand sailor; all provided information for this project. Peter O'Neill and the crew of *Mary T,* Sigmund and Carol Baardsen, who were caught in the Queens Birthday storm between New Zealand and Tonga, shared more of their stories with us for this edition of the book. To all we give a sincere Thank You.

Helen Meier took the photographs of the authors that appear on the back cover of this book. Steve Callahan, editor of *Cruising World* Magazine and survivor of an amazing month-and-a-half-long drift across the Atlantic in his life raft, took the time to do a careful and thoughtful analysis of this book. His suggestions are reflected in this second printing.

Waterline Books in England and its editor Peter Coles have encouraged us as we did the editing for this second printing in preparation for a British edition. Geoff Pack, editor of *Yachting Monthly UK,* has also encouraged us and provided information.

During early 1995 we visited the United Sates and presented seminars to almost 6,000 people. This handbook, in a less-than-formal form, was used during these seminars. We would like to thank the

ACKNOWLEDGMENTS

sailors we spoke with for their input and encouragement. It is because of their enthusiasm that we have gone on with the project instead of kicking back in the sun and solitude of the islands of Ihla Grande, Brazil.

Also during our North American trip, several people helped us gather information and coordinate the project. My brother, Allen Zatkin, and his wife, Marcia, put up with telephone and fax messages arriving at all sorts of strange hours, as we contacted people in both New Zealand and England for further information. My mother, Marion Dryer, served as a mail drop during our wandering. And Gingerlee Field McMicken and Ray McMicken invited us to live in their delightful guest cottage to complete the editing on this project. It is difficult to give these special family members enough thanks.

Finally, we would like to thank a man named Sam. We met him only once, in Townsville, Queensland, Australia. But he went out of his way to let us know that the article we wrote in 1982 for SAIL Magazine (which is reprinted here) served as a guide on his Alejula 38 for him when he hit the first big storm of his cruising life. "It worked just like you said it would, so keep on writing about heaving-to. It's like magic, you can't believe how that slick calms things down until you see it." Sam's words have been at the back of our minds as we wrote this handbook.

Preface

Anyone can take the helm when the sea is calm." So goes an old saying, and it carries the implication that it takes a very special kind of person to take that same helm when the sea puts on an unkind aspect.

This notion is understandable, considering the intensity of an ocean storm. Dial in the possibility of rocks under your lee, and the impossibility of respite or shelter and you begin to see why the sea can give pause even to stalwart souls, and can dissuade most people from venturing out in anything smaller than a "love boat."

It's an unfortunate situation and basically an unnecessary one; well-designed, well-equipped sailboats are, by definition, capable of dealing with almost anything the ocean can dish out. As Joseph Conrad put it, a good boat "like a seabird going to rest upon the angry waves...will lay out the heaviest gale that ever made you doubt living long enough to see another sunrise."

But that boat needs a well-designed, well-equipped crew. It needs people who have sound, effective, thoroughly rehearsed means of coping with dangerous weather. It does not need the mishmash of speculation, ritual, and knocking-on-wood that too often masquerades as storm tactics.

There are many vessels lost at sea each year, for the same reasons that cause most accidents; varying combinations of bad equipment and bad judgment. But we are not helpless in the face of these problems. Appropriate behavior makes all the difference.

In the following pages you'll find hard-won, carefully distilled information on what constitutes appropriate behavior in a storm. Not to say there is any magic wand here. If you spend any time at sea, you'll spend some time wishing you were someplace else. But the amazing truth is that those times can be some of the best of your life, a tempering process that nourishes and confirms the resilience of the human spirit. Prepare for it, train for it, and you'll find it's also true that anyone can take the helm when the sea is high.

—Brion Toss, Author, *Rigger's Apprentice*

Table of Contents

Introduction

Storm-force winds blew through the conversation as we sat on the breeze-cooled tenth-floor balcony of our friends' Rio de Janeiro apartment. Mara Blumer and Helio Viana had created a gathering of local sailors, each of whom had built their own 29- to 35-foot cruising boats and dreamed of going off exploring in the near future. The special guest was Roberto Barros, the man who had designed their boats. He is a rarity in the world of yacht designers, because he and his wife have made adventuresome high-latitude and tropical voyages in two different boats, a 26-footer and a 28-footer.

"My crew and I hove-to for two days near the Falkland Islands during a strong storm because we didn't want to lose all the miles we had worked so hard to gain," Roberto told us. "We were not exactly comfortable, but we felt safe, and no waves broke over my fin-keeled spade rudder boat," he said, as he described how he'd backed the staysail and tightened in his heavily reefed mainsail. "If the wind had gotten worse I don't know what we would have done next; the books I read say we would have needed to run off. We'd have lost all those miles."

Earlier that same day Larry and I had received extensive notes regarding seven crews who had abandoned their boats when a storm swept through an 80-boat-strong cruising/rally fleet bound north out of New Zealand as winter approached (SAIL Magazine, October 1994). An eighth, a modern 40-footer, was lost with all hands. All of the boats that suffered damage had been running or lying-ahull during the storm, and when the survivors were interviewed, a common thread weaving through their comments was, "I wish I had known more about how to heave-to."

Over the past 35 years, for reasons we can only guess at, heaving-to, the vital safety valve used by commercial and pleasure sailors on all sorts and sizes of vessels for centuries, has been gradually discounted by most yachting writers and teachers, until many of today's sailors either know little about it, or feel "it won't work on modern boats."

As our discussion progressed on that Rio de Janeiro balcony, Roberto said something that made us realize one of the problems, "If heaving-to is more than backing a staysail and sheeting in a deeply reefed main, how would you describe it?"

Larry answered, "In moderate winds, maybe even in winds up to gale force, you've described one of the many ways you can get a boat to heave-to. But when winds top that, it means using any sail combination, any gear combination necessary to get your boat to lie stopped, about 50 degrees from the wind and drifting slowly, directly away from the wind behind its own slick [turbulence]. Only if you create a good slick and stay behind it can you break the power of the seas." Larry then told how he'd learned about the details of this method when he first read books by Captain J.C. Voss, who had used an old-style canvas cone-type sea anchor with manila line to assist his riding sail as he hove-to during his small-boat voyages. Voss had written the most concise description we've ever read regarding these principles in his book, *The Venturesome Voyages of Captain Voss.** "We modern sailors are more fortunate than Voss," Larry went on. "We have extremely durable nylon parachute-type sea anchors and stretchy nylon anchor lines, stronger storm sails to keep our modern fin and skeg-type boat lying properly hove-to."

"But," Roberto interrupted, "you have said something important; you are not just heaving-to. You are adding a third element to the equation, and I have never read about that."

What he says is not surprising. Over the past 30 years Larry and I have been gathering information on heavy-weather tactics, and we have found only two books describing the use of heaving-to with the assistance of a large drogue—one old, one new.** Descriptions of heaving-to elsewhere are largely limited to the stock answer Roberto gave. So it is little wonder there is confusion on this matter.

Larry in some ways was very fortunate. He came in to the sailing life when the majority of books describing ocean voyaging were written by commercial sailors such as Voss, Allan Villiers, Captain Worsley, and Frank Bullen. So he started with heaving-to as the basis of his storm planning. His faith in this method was reinforced by his good fortune in being first mate under a top professional delivery skipper, schooner captain and practitioner of heaving-to, the late Bob Sloan. Bob logged over 500,000 miles under sail and introduced Larry to the second-hand military ordinance parachutes used as sea anchors by the commercial tuna fishermen of Southern Mexico and California.

"If I didn't think there was something I could do to get a rest during a storm, some way I could affect the waves and sap their power," Larry told me, "I wouldn't cross oceans in small boats." He used these words to lure me gently into ocean voyaging. Then he chose as my inauguration into his life Mexican coastal cruises, where gale-force winds are rare. Only as my confidence grew did we set off across oceans and into areas where stronger winds and bigger seas could be expected. After experiencing several gales at sea, when we both felt confident of our boat and our heavy-weather tactics, we began voyaging to higher latitudes, where the likelihood of encountering storms was increased. Each of these encounters have furthered my belief that heaving-to or lying-to a parachute-type sea anchor is far safer than running. This was doubly reinforced with the worst storm of our career: An unseasonable typhoon rammed up against a ridge of high pressure

**The Venturesome Voyages of Captain Voss*
***Drag Device Data Base,* by Victor Shane, see bibliography

INTRODUCTION

and caught us near Australia's Great Barrier Reef. We were forced to lie-to a parachute anchor for over 56 hours in winds exceeding 70 knots. (Weather forecasters spoke of winds to 85 in our area.) Wind blew against current in only 100 fathoms of water, creating breaking seas, which forced 400-foot freighters to heave-to. We have never before seen waves dangerous enough to stop ships. We could see two of them nearby, maneuvering to keep their bows into the seas for over 12 hours. Yet even in seas like this we were able to bring *Taleisin* through with the only damage limited to chafed lines, chafed nerves, and bruised bodies. Other sailors within 50 miles of us faired far worse; two lost their lives while using other tactics.

This experience reinforced our belief that choosing the correct storm tactic is vital if you encounter difficult situations. What one sailor using one tactic calls a survival storm another who used a different tactic may describe as a real tough blow. The difference is that once a sea knocks the boat flat, once a boat or crew suffers damage, fear may set in and imagination take over, causing morale to drop and storm intensity appear to increase. As you read further in these pages you'll see other examples in which one boat near the center of a storm system was settled into a hove-to position and survived with no damage, while the same storm sank or rolled nearby boats whose crews chose to run or lie-ahull.

For several years we have felt hesitant about writing a text on storm sailing. It is difficult to be sure we have done the research necessary to show every wrinkle, every move that will make heaving-to work for the variety of boats out cruising today. Furthermore, the use of large drogues such as para-anchors is undergoing an evolutionary process. Also, different gear and techniques are used for monohulls from those used for multihulls. Our Brazilian friends' comments and those of the sailors in New Zealand's rally fleet make it clear that these words are needed. An additional goal to get us putting something down on paper comes from Patience Wales, editor of SAIL Magazine, who urged us to update two articles we wrote on storm management and heaving-to back in 1982. But there is more to this topic than we could easily condense into one or two articles. So we have put this handbook together as the beginning of what we see as an evolutionary project; it is not the end product. The first section of the handbook consists of the articles from 1982 which we also used as an appendix in two of the books we wrote about our first cruises on 24-foot, 7-inch, 5-ton *Seraffyn,* telling of her 11-year circumnavigation. Also included are the stories that prompted the original articles. This is followed by a question-and-answer format update to include information gathered from a further 12 years of voyaging on 29-foot, 6-inch, 8.5-ton *Taleisin,* as well as during yacht deliveries and races and while testing heaving-to and parachute drogue usage on modern fin-and-skeg racer/cruisers off South Africa's infamous False Bay, Capetown Provence. Also included is information from interviews with people who have had to try out storm tactics in the big tank, where there are no scientific controls, just reality.

There are no discussions of more obvious rough weather gear here, such as flares, harnesses, EPIRBs, etc. All of these are well covered in other texts, such as those in the bibliography. We want this handbook to be a down-to-it, meat-and-potatoes discussion of what you can do to prepare for and face storms. Therefore, the third section is a series of checklists you can use as guidelines for boat choice, gear preparation, crew preparation, and at sea—preparation for times when the barometer starts to drop and wind strengths go up.

The methods discussed in this workbook could be just as important for the family on a trailer-sailer bound from Long Beach to Catalina or a J/24 crossing Lake Mead, or a sharpie skiff exploring the coast of Maine, as they are for offshore sailors. By using the simple gear that should be already on board, you could safely ride out an unexpected storm and gain the confidence and respect of your family and crew. The same methods can also be used to stabilize the situation if you suffer a gear failure such as losing your rudder or mast in more normal strength winds. Heaving-to or using a jib as a sea anchor will help you hang on to your searoom while you effect repairs, reef sails, store gear, or pull your dinghy on board.

Big boat, small boat, onshore, offshore—if after you have read this workbook you still feel running before a storm is theoretically the best tactic, it is nonetheless vitally important to learn about heaving-to. There is no guarantee your storm will catch you when you have a lot of searoom to run in. If an inhospitable lee shore lies only 50 or even 100 miles downwind, you have to be prepared and know how to heave-to. Running onto a storm-swept rocky shore or wave-pounded coral reef is not an option.

Section I—Storm Management

We originally wrote about storm management and storm tactic choices in our books Seraffyn's *Oriental Adventures* and Seraffyn's *European Adventure*. The information contained in their appendices gives a fair picture of what we have learned about storm tactics during our first 11-year voyage (1969–1980). So we have included them in this handbook in their original form. To give a better picture of how our thinking developed, we have included stories from the bodies of those books and also from *Cruising in* Seraffyn. Please be patient as you read this section, for we know you will find some of your questions unanswered. That is why the next section of this handbook developed. In it we will include information we have gathered as we voyaged further on *Taleisin* (1983 to present) and on other boats we sailed on.

Storms and Cruising

Like most sailors returning from an extended cruise, we enjoy chatting with would-be voyagers. Invariably these conversations start off with "How did you cut loose, what kind of boat, what kind of equipment?" But as the evening progresses, one subject starts to dominate the conversation: storms, tactics, storm gear. This fascination with the power of the sea and wind gone wild has made Adlard Coles's *Heavy Weather Sailing* one of the best-selling nautical books in history. It has also frightened some potential voyagers so much that the pleasure goes out of sailing. Each time these inexperienced people leave the breakwater, they wonder, if the sea is this lumpy in a force-six wind, what's it like in a full gale? a storm? a hurricane?

The first thing to remember is that storms represent only a small percentage of your actual, at-sea sailing time. During our eleven-year circumnavigation on board *Seraffyn,* we spent approximately 10,600 hours at sea. We sailed over a slightly unusual route, which included a detour to England and the Baltic, another to the north end of the Adriatic, and a particularly stormy passage across the North Pacific from Japan to Canada. So we probably encountered more stormy weather than the average sailor would during a well-planned voyage to the South Pacific. During our time on *Seraffyn* we encountered twenty gales and storms that required using storm tactics. We lay hove-to for approximately 300 hours with winds of force eight and above during that eleven-year period, and almost 120 of that was during our forty-nine-day passage from Japan to Victoria, British Columbia. That works out to 3.5 percent of our sailing hours. Then, when you figure we spent an average of only 960 hours per year at sea, or about 11 percent of our cruising life, that means less than thirty hours a year were spent handling the special mental and physical problems of heavy-weather sailing. If we add the time we spent delivering other people's yachts, the averages do go up. But this is because yacht delivery is a business. We can't choose where we sail or when we set sail. Within reason we go where the owner pays us to go. Since owners want to enjoy the very best season right to the limit, it's not surprising that delivery teams end up hitting a higher average of rough weather.*

If storms are the main concern you have as a cruising sailor, compare them to the danger that commuters accept as they drive along the freeways to work each day. They have to worry about other people taking drugs, talking on cellphones, or drinking, then driving. Com-

*Since writing this appendix, we have sailed almost 40,000 miles on *Taleisin,* including a west-about passage south of Tasmania and westward, below 40 degrees south across the Australian Bight, a voyage around the South of Africa, plus delivery trips on various yachts in the Pacific and Tasman Sea. We have accumulated about 1,650 days actually at sea, or 39,600 hours. During this time we have been in storm-force winds for 31 days, gale-force winds 59 days. This equals about 5.5 percent of our sailing time, a relatively high average for cruising sailors. But it must be remembered that this includes 5 passages across the Tasman Sea, an area known for its boisterousness.

muters expose themselves to danger probably 300 hours each year, or ten times as often as the average cruiser faces gale-force winds. The fatal-accident rate on the freeway is alarming; even worse is the justifiable fear of maiming. But the psychological impact of a storm at sea is far greater, because we all accept freeway driving as normal. It is difficult to imagine or experience storms at sea, and you have to handle them all alone. I think it is this feeling of being completely responsible for your own fate and that of your crew that creates both the worst and the best feelings of being at sea. As a storm approaches you begin to worry: Is the boat properly prepared, did I equip it right, how bad is the blow actually going to be? During the actual blow, these fears are shoved somewhat to the back of your mind as you become occupied by the work of protecting yourself and the boat. Then, when the storm shows the first signs of letting up, when the first patch of blue shows through the clouds, a feeling of elation starts to grow. You did it! Alone out there, you met a test and passed it. If there were any ways of shortening the first stages of this reaction, storms could be accepted more easily.

The first time Larry and I sailed into a full-fledged storm, we had no warning at all. We had just skittered across the infamous Gulf of Tehuantepec, on Mexico's southwestern flank. We'd missed the famous blasting winds that blow there five days of every winter month. Then, as we crossed the imaginary boundary into Nicaraguan waters, 150 miles offshore of the Gulf of Papagayo, we noticed a squall ahead. We reefed. The squall hit. Within an hour it built to a gale that lasted for three days and often grew to full storm strength. The few weather reports we were able to pick up did not report these winds until a day after they started. Our barometer had climbed only slightly, that's all. We did what was necessary, set the sea anchor, cursed the wind, and waited. We had no time to worry about what might happen; we just acted. This was in complete contrast to the typhoon that hit us as we crossed the Bay of Bengal. All of the classic signs began to appear almost three days before the wind increased. We both worried, planned, checked our gear, and worried. Even though we had ten years of experience between our first storm and this one, we were no more prepared than during the Gulf of Papagayo storm. We still had to depend on the same equipment and plans we made before we set sail.

Noise is probably the most unnerving part of a storm. If you've been fortunate enough to experience a few blows while your boat lies secure in a well-sheltered harbor, you'll be a bit more prepared for the whine and howl of wind and rigging. Brian Cooke, a well-experienced cruising friend, said the worst problem with mast steps is that they increase the rigging noise during heavy winds to the point where he found that if he was below decks he overestimated wind speeds by two or three forces. His mast steps also set up a humming that vibrated through the whole boat and added an unnerving note to the sounds of stinging spray, crumbling seas, and shifting canned goods. One of the first things we do when the boat is lying safely hove-to is track down every extraneous noise we can. We tie the halyards away from the mast, pad the pots and pans, find any clunking cans. Once the unnecessary noises are cut out, I find I begin to accept the other sounds as more natural until they fade into the background, especially when I begin to remember that noise can't hurt us. In fact, neither can the wind. It's green waves breaking against the boat that matter, motion that can represent real danger.

There is no doubt that gales at sea can leave your body feeling bruised and tired. No matter how seakindly your boat is, oddball waves can give it a jerk that will catch you or crew members off-balance. Yet the natural survival instincts that seem to live inside all human beings surface most completely during a storm. Larry has earned some cuts on his hands from handling gear on a bucking deck. I've gotten some good black-and-blue marks. But the irregularity of the motion during a storm seems to act as a constant reminder: "Be careful, be careful." On the other hand, we know of several incidents where people were injured after a storm, and that includes me. As soon as we set sail after lying hove-to in the North Sea off England, I forgot to hold on, the boat lurched, and I cracked my tailbone.

A question we've often been asked is "Wouldn't you feel safer on a larger boat?" Since we've had the fortunate (or unfortunate, according to how you look at it) experience of being at sea during gales on various boats ranging from *Seraffyn*'s 24 feet to an 85-foot schooner, we can say that the smaller boat has certain advantages, if not in physical comfort, then definitely in mental security. First, the gear is easier and lighter to handle, so we are less reluctant to set storm sails, sea anchors, or reefs. Second, the spaces involved are smaller, so moving around on deck and below during the height of a blow is easier. A trip from the bunk to the galley across a 54-footer with 16 feet of beam was harder than the same trip on an 11-foot-wide 35-footer. Handholds are farther apart on the larger boat. Third, it's easier to inspect and maintain all of the gear and parts on a smaller boat, so there is more peace of mind and less concern about technical failures. Finally, if things go wrong, if your reefed main splits, if your boom leaps out of the gallows, if an anchor gets loose on the foredeck, if you have to dig out and set the trysail, it is easier and safer to get the smaller boat under control.

The actual motion of a boat in a storm is affected by displacement and design far more than it is by length. Certain hull shapes are more seakindly. A small, moderately heavy boat with a long keel, one-third ballast ratio, and low topsides can feel better in a gale than a fin-keeled 50 percent ballasted, light-displacement boat with high topsides that is twice as long.

Beyond design considerations, the thing that most affects your boat's motion in gale conditions is the tactic you choose to use. During our North Pacific crossing from Japan, 10 full-fledged storms decided to race us. Six of them won, and in five cases we lay well inside the storm radius (sustained winds from 50 to 55 knots). My reaction was anger. I took to my bunk and hid in a book. Larry, on the other hand, got bored, then curious. After heaving-to for the first 12-hour blow, he decided to try other methods of storm management recommended by small-boat voyagers. We ran for 6 hours with one storm when the winds were going our way. We had to assist the wind-vane steering, so one of us had to be in the cockpit at all times. Our memory of broaching when we ran during a storm in the Baltic kept eating at our confidence. Once the seas grew and began to crumble, the boat's motion was squirrelly and irregular. Sleeping below decks was very difficult; steering was tiring. In short, if we had to continue running with the storm before it began to lose strength, we would have grown very tired. Continued running seemed a sure course to the bad decisions or tired helmsmanship that exhaustion can bring on.

The next storm that blasted through tempted Larry to try lying ahull, that is, taking down all sail and letting the boat take care of itself. We have never been so uncomfortable in a storm. For the first time ever, a sea broke on deck with such force that it moved our deck box a quarter of an inch, shifting four five-sixteenths-inch silicon bronze bolts to do so. The motion became so severe that we actually began wondering if this could be our ultimate storm. When that wave hit us like a ton of bricks, Larry decided to get out and do something. He set the triple-reefed mainsail, tied the helm to leeward, and *Seraffyn* lay hove-to. I couldn't believe the difference. The boat seemed to stop fighting the waves, her motion evened out, the horrid rolling stopped, and in fact life inside the boat felt so much more comfortable that I got out of my bunk and made up a pot of scrambled eggs with fried spam and a cabbage salad to welcome Larry back below.

During the next three storms, we hove-to, trying various sail combinations, and finally hove-to using the sea anchor as described by Larry in the following appendix. *Seraffyn* suffered no damage; we felt relatively comfortable. At no time did we worry about survival, nor did we ship any seas, only spray.

Fortunately, storms normally do not last for more than 24 hours, except in high latitudes during winter seasons. Whenever we have read of people running with a storm for days on end, we've studied their situation as best we could from weather charts. In most of these situations, it appeared that the storm would have passed over the hapless sailor much sooner if he or she had stopped moving forward. When you consider that most storms move at between 6 and 9 knots following the major currents of the world, if you run at 6 knots, you could stay in the storm. If, on the other hand, you stop, the average storm with a 150-mile-wide storm radius could pass over you in one day. This could be a way of cutting your storm time down. But the best tactic of all is to try to avoid storms.

There definitely are safer voyaging routes to take, safer times to sail. The pilot charts compiled by the U.S. Hydrographic Office or the British Admiralty are the first step toward planning a voyage with low storm chances. Combine this information with the weather data given in Ocean Passages for the World (British Admiralty) and the pilot book for your voyaging area, and you'll begin to form a better picture of what to expect along the way. We have found it pays to study the weather information for a three-month period rather than for just one month. If the incidence of storms seems to increase toward the end of the third month, plan to get under way sooner; if the three-month trend is toward a major change, such as from the northeast monsoon to the southwest monsoon, leave early again. We learned the hard way that monsoons can change before they are supposed to. We wallowed in the middle of the Arabian Sea and had a normal 20-day passage stretch until it lasted for 36 days. Then we were late on our voyage plan and set off across the Bay of Bengal when the chance of gale-force winds shown on the pilot chart increased from less than one day a month to three a month. That's when we hit the side of a typhoon.

Another thing we've learned the hard way is to avoid the axis of major currents. Even though it is tempting to grab the free lift offered by the Gulf Stream, you increase your chances of meeting unusual weather patterns and rougher seas. Winston Bushnell described how his boat *Dove* was rolled 360 degrees during a storm in the axis of Agulhas current off South Africa. He lost his mast and rudder, but, with the help of his wife and two daughters, he jury-rigged the boat and sailed into port two hundred miles on. When they arrived, they found that other racing yachtsmen had been in the same storm but outside the axis of the current. Their description of the sea condition was "probably gale force," while the Bushnells experienced hurricane-sized seas driven into confusion by an opposing 4-knot current.

Both warm and cold currents can create another major sailing hazard, one we learned about when we foolishly grabbed a chance to ride the Kuroshio current north from Taiwan to Japan. Heavy fog! The difference between air temperature and water temperature causes it. Add fog to gale-force winds and 3 knots of current, dozens of steep-to islands plus heavy shipping, and you have the formula that gave Larry most of the white hair around his temples.

Good weather reports offshore can warn you of approaching storms. You could possibly alter course and avoid the storm centers; you could prepare the boat a bit more. Unfortunately, there are few comprehensive reports with long-range weather predictions for areas that people prefer to cruise in. WWV has an hourly synopsis of what is already happening with the weather in each major sea area. The reports are updated every 6 hours and trace the movement of any major storms. But none of this information gives you more than two or three days' warning, and the storm tracks cannot be accurately predicted. So, after you've planned as best you can, it pays to depend less on the radio weather forecasts and study your barometer, along with a good book on weather predicting. We've found that Alan Watts's *Instant Weather Forecasting* has helped us become almost as accurate in predicting major long-term increases in wind-speed as any radio reports. The twenty or so color photographs of clouds and simple instructions have seemed to work everywhere we've sailed. Since our observations take in local signs, we can combine them with any information we have about large highs or depressions, then come up with storm predictions often before the radio lists them.

Even with the best of planning, the best of weather reports, if you make ocean passages, you are going to encounter a gale or storm at sea eventually. We gathered every bit of information we could about the best time for a passage from Japan to Canada. We studied every chart, and all of the averages showed gales one day a month maximum along our whole route. We had six storms. The West Coast of the United States had the wettest, stormiest summer in history. It even rained in Death Valley! So before you leave you must prepare yourself and your boat for storm conditions. One of the most important considerations besides a well-constructed, leak-free hull, deck, and cabin is the size of the port lights or windows. The smaller the better. Even if you build your cabin ports triple-strong, remember that something could break them. It wouldn't be impossible to cover up the hole left when a 5-by-8-inch port light glass broke. But if it were a 24-by-18-inch window, that would be another matter. High coamings that increase the volume of your cockpit and trap water so that it funnels down your companionway should be avoided. In reality, even 2-inch-diameter cockpit drains work too slowly when a boat is dipping and plunging in a seaway. If your boat has angled drop boards (i.e., the top of the companionway opening is wider than the bottom), arrange some kind of lock that can work both from inside and outside the cabin. This type of drop board is easier to use under normal conditions, but if a sea fills the cockpit, the angled board has to lift only a bit to come loose and float away.

Good handholds both on deck and below are imperative. If you store a hard dinghy on deck upside down, put handholds on the bottom of it. They'll also act as skids to save the dinghy wear and tear on the shore. Good lifelines, good nonskid decks, strong lash-downs for everything above and below decks including your floorboards all add to your mental and physical security during a storm. Lee cloths are another important consideration. We prefer cloths to leeboards because they contour to your body and feel more comfortable. It's surprising how you can dose off even during the height of a storm if you feel sure you can't be tossed out of your bunk, yet don't get bruised each time the boat lurches.

STORM MANAGEMENT

Keep your deck area clear of items that could become lethal flying objects. A delivery skipper we know was caught in a severe storm in northern latitudes when he had to move a race boat early in the season. The 60-foot boat was running before the storm when it rolled and lost its mast. A 55-gallon drum of diesel fuel got loose on deck and smashed the leg of one of the crew. Even though the skipper was able to rig a temporary antenna and contact help through the ham net, it took four days for a rescue vessel to reach them because of the rough conditions. This particular incident has often reminded us that there are very few good reasons to store heavy items on deck during a passage. A few plastic 5-gallon jugs are one thing, but the motorcycles, fuel drums, and portable generators we've seen on some cruising boats are another.

The special gear you need just for storms is reasonably inexpensive and easy to store: a storm trysail, a storm staysail or jib, a parachute-style sea anchor, and chafing gear to protect any lines you use. A general consensus of voyagers seems to be that cutters under 28 feet long can usually use an extra strongly built mainsail with three reefs as a storm trysail. We did just that on *Seraffyn*. On the other hand, when we waited too long before replacing that mainsail, it blew out during a storm, and only good fortune kept it from ripping to shreds. So, if you choose to sail without a trysail, replace your mainsail sooner rather than later. Sloops and boats over 28 feet need a separate storm trysail. With a sloop rig, your sail area keeps moving forward as you reef and reduce your jib size until the center of effort moves too far forward. Then the boat develops lee helm and cannot work to windward. A sloop probably won't heave-to unless you have a trysail. On larger boats it is hard to build a single sail that is strong enough to take the strains of serving as a storm trysail yet light enough for medium winds. Our new 30-footer will have a trysail with a separate track that extends quite close to the deck. That way, we can hank the trysail in place and leave it sitting bagged on deck, ready to use. If it is there we might hoist it as soon as we need it. Not only will that be easier than hoisting it at the height of blow, but it could also save some wear and strain on our regular mainsail.*

We've heard of some sailors who have gates in their sail track and plan to hank their trysail in place above the regular mainsail. This seems a bit more difficult and possibly dangerous, since you have to reach quite high up the mast to get the slides in place. Slightly better is a separate track from deck level to just above the furled mainsail, where a switch gate leads the trysail slides onto the main track. This system presents one major problem. This gate can become misaligned or stuck when you need it most.

Sea anchors have changed since Slocum's day. Modern materials and research by the navy have turned this previously hard-to-stow, undependable item into an easy-to-handle, easy-to-maintain unit.

*Trysails and trysail track installation are discussed in detail in Section V.

Instead of being a relatively small, rot-prone canvas cone with a metal loop, a modern sea anchor can be made of nylon mesh and shaped like a parachute. On *Seraffyn* we used a standard 8-foot-diameter para-anchor that cost $35 at a navy-surplus store. We did remove the trip line that was with the standard para-anchor because it seemed to foul the whole works. Bringing the para-anchor in after a blow didn't seem too much more difficult without it, since we could use our anchor windlass. Many fishermen on the West Coast buy these sea anchors and use them to hold position while they get some sleep on breezy nights. We use our second anchor rode, 300 feet of 5/8-inch nylon line, as the para-anchor line. The only other item we carry for storm use is a galvanized 3/8-inch swivel to attach the para-anchor to its rode.

The hardest part of preparing for the storms you'll eventually meet at sea is getting practice before you set off. No one wants to let loose from their moorings when the forecasters talk of gales and rain. But this is when you should get out and try battening down your hatches, fitting your storm windows in place, working with your wet-weather gear on. If you wait until your first offshore storm to set your trysail, you might find that systems that worked fine in harbor don't quite serve with wind and seas thrown into the equation. By going out in strong winds and heaving-to, you'll figure out what combination of sails and rudder angle works best. Even if it is daytime, climb into your bunk and see if your lee cloths will let you lie comfortably. Practice setting your sea anchor and retrieving it. If you are outfitting your boat in an inland sailing area such as the Great Lakes, you'll find it difficult to recreate the conditions of a full gale at sea, where waves begin to form into regular large patterns, so setting a sea anchor and understanding how it works will be difficult. But the experience of moving about in strong winds will be invaluable. Once you've practiced, you'll be able to store away your storm equipment and inspect it once a year just as you do your medical kit.

Storms at sea are a very small part of the experience of most cruisers. The photographs of freak waves shown in Adlard Coles's book on heavy-weather sailing were taken in the North Atlantic during mid-winter. The only dangerous sea we encountered in 11 years of cruising and 16 years of delivering yachts was in the Baltic a month after the end of the normal yachting season. The percentage of cruising sailors encountering more than physical discomfort, minor gear failures, and normal apprehension during storms offshore is minuscule compared to the losses and injuries suffered by cruisers hitting reefs and rocks or dragging anchor. There's no doubt that once you set off for a long cruise you are eventually going to hit storm-force winds. If you and your boat are well prepared, you'll come through the experience feeling prouder and more confident. You'll also find you soon forget the experience as your mind focuses on the hundreds of more enjoyable aspects of offshore cruising.

Some Thoughts on Heavy Weather

B ut in running before it your vessel may go along quite comfortably and dry for some time, and then with dreadful suddenness, a sea may come over the stern and put you and your
ship out of business....
—Captain Voss, *The Venturesome Voyages of Captain Voss*

A few years ago *Tzu Hang* was running from Reykhavik to the northwest point of Iceland in a southwest gale. It was a dark night and the
wind Force 9 with a heavy sea on her quarter. *Tzu Hang* had only
her storm headsail set and in order to prevent it jibing over and back
again, with sudden strains on sheet, halyard, and stay, we were running with the wind on our quarter, which gave us a nice offing from
the inhospitable shore. *Tzu Hang* was tearing along through the
night in the conditions that she seems to like best, and I was happy
and singing at the tiller, since we were going fast in the direction we
wished to go. Suddenly I felt, rather than saw, a monster wave
breathing down my neck and coming at a slightly different angle.
The next moment we were hit with a shock that felt as if a ten-ton
lorry had run into us. *Tzu Hang* was knocked bodily sideways and
the tiller was wrenched out of my hand and thumped against the leeward coaming at the limit of its travel....*Tzu Hang*'s masts went down
to the horizontal....

[In another instance] *Tzu Hang* was running before a gale
which I should estimate now to have been Force 10 or more. At no
time was she running too fast, nor was she particularly difficult to
steer....When she pitchpoled a very high and exceptionally steep
wave hit her, considerably higher than she was long. It must have
broken as she assumed an almost vertical position on its face. The
movement was extremely violent and quick. There was no sensation
of being in a dangerous position with disaster threatening. Disaster
was suddenly there.
—Miles Smeeton, *Because the Horn is There*

It was becoming more and more difficult to hold *Joshua* before the
seas because the trailing hawsers made her less and less maneuver-
able as the seas got bigger. She was yawing more even with the helm
right down, and what I had vaguely feared eventually happened. But
it was my fault, for my attention must have momentarily wandered
after fifteen hours at the helm. Carried by a wave *Joshua* suddenly
came beam on to the seas and when the breaker arrived it was too
late. A rush of icy water hit me in the neck and the next moment
Joshua was heeled rapidly over. The angle of the heel increased
steadily but not abruptly while noise became dim. Then the

silence was suddenly broken by the unholy din of a cascade of objects flying across the cabin...three or four seconds...then *Joshua* righted herself.

[Later that night] the boat was running exactly stern on to a fast approaching wave, nicely curved but not excessively large, on the point of breaking...or maybe not breaking...I was wide awake, I think I was even extra lucid at that moment.

The stern lifted as always and then, accelerating suddenly but without heeling the slightest, *Joshua* buried her forward part in the sea at an angle of about 30 degrees, as far as the forward edge of the coachroof. Half the boat was under water. Almost immediately she emerged again....We had almost been pitchpoled by a slightly hesitant wave—I would not have believed it possible.

—Bernard Moitessier, *The First Voyage of the* Joshua

Our technique for the entire period of storms was to run with the prevailing wind and wave set on the starboard quarter, holding a fair course and surging down the faces of the rising swells. As the crests caught us, they would kick the stern over, and *Sorcery* would round up slightly till she luffed; then she would fly along the top of the wave....Steering was never difficult in these gale conditions, but it did require some concentration and by the tenth day of real wind, everyone on board had put in many hours of heavy-weather helm time....Then the freight train hit us. There was no time to react. As the starboard locker emptied onto me, the engine, which had been battery charging, kicked off. I pile-drived into the amazingly white surface of the overhead, right where the cabin sole used to be; then the port lockers emptied out. Sometime in between it seemed that a wave had washed through into the forepeak, but I barely noticed it....the first definite sounds that penetrated the chaos were the piercing screams from on deck, then a shout of "Man overboard!"

—Aulan Fitzpatrick, "360 Degree Roll Sweeps *Sorcery* Clean," Sail, August 1976.

All Monday it was staysail only. To hold the course without flogging its 300 square feet in accidental gybes required constant attention at the helm....[The wind was an estimated] Force 9, over 46 knots....And so dawned the fateful morning...the wind had veered. We'd come over onto the port gybe....We remarked the abating seas; at the same time our pace diminished to eight knots. "Were we racing," I said, "We'd be upping the main." We agreed in the interest of rest and comfort to postpone this until I came on watch again at 1300....

Bill had impressed me as an alert helmsman more than once in the past ten days. I could see him through the companionway checking the tillermaster [electric autopilot]....I read the first sentence of the first six volumes of Anthony Trollope. Then Bill shouted,

STORM MANAGEMENT

"Look out..."

A second to rise up, another to swing my legs off the bunk. Four seconds. Bill's next agonized cry coincided with the creaking slapping sound of a flat surface slamming water with maximum impact....

Even as the mast must have struck the water and *Streamer* lay like a wing crippled swan on her side I still felt confident....A second shattering smack. Then gently as the mast subsided below the surface the bunk revolved above my head. I stood calf deep in water in the cabin ceiling.

[Later Bill told me] "I'd been looking ahead. I turned around. This wall. Forty feet high. It had two crests just off the stern. I kicked tilly clear. Grabbed the wheel and pulled her off with all my weight. Three spokes. I thought she'd come back until I saw the mast hit the water. Then the second crest hit us."—Philip S. Weld, "Five Nights Upside Down—Then Rescue for *Gulf Streamer*," Sail, August 1976.

Seraffyn's broach as described in the story from Seraffyn's *European Adventure:* Broach on page 47 was a classic case of running too long under bare poles.

Seven different instances, five very different types of boats. *Seraffyn* is 24 feet long with short overhangs and heavy displacement. *Gulf Streamer* is a 60-foot-long lightweight trimaran. *Sorcery* is a 61-foot-long light-displacement IOR racing boat. *Joshua* is a 40-foot double-ended heavy steel ketch. *Tzu Hang* is a 46-foot-long wooden canoe stern ketch. Each encountered waves that could have been disastrous, yet only two of these instances happened near Cape Horn. Smeeton's first account was near Iceland. *Sorcery* got into trouble in the North Pacific, *Gulf Streamer* in the North Atlantic, and *Seraffyn* in the Baltic. All of us got into trouble while running, with no warning and with dreadful suddenness.

Why do yachtsmen continue to run in heavy weather? It's because they are not aware of any danger. The yacht feels as if it is completely under control. In some instances it is even being steered by vane or autopilot. The motion is relatively comfortable. The wind speed seems lower because you are running away from it. To round up and heave-to means a definite decision, backed by action and hard work. It means setting some sort of riding sail, sea anchor, or drogue. Rounding up to heave-to can be frightening, especially if you have left it too long. And that's what happens. You hang on longer than is prudent, hoping the wind and sea will lie down. That's usually when disaster strikes.

Heaving-to requires gear preparation before leaving port. It requires experimentation to learn the adjustment and trimming of sails and/or drogues necessary to get your particular boat into the proper hove-to position. Every boat heaves-to differently, and the only way to learn which way works best for yours is to practice at sea in winds of gale force. Few of us choose to go out in heavy winds just to practice. It is easier to accept a pat solution like running under bare poles, with or without warps or drogues. We have been lulled into a false sense of security by other yachtsmen who have fortunately survived to write about "running with it."

In the author's notes in his book *The First Voyage of the* Joshua, Bernard Moitessier says, "The following lines are only a very incomplete testimony, and perhaps quite mistaken. Just because we have once got away without suffering damage I cannot pretend to talk like an authority on the handling of a yacht in the high latitudes of the South Pacific."

Miles Smeeton makes a similar statement in *Because the Horn is There*: "I write of the management of a ship in heavy weather with hesitation, because my experience, although gained in many seas, is confined to one ship."

These men don't profess to be authorities on heavy weather. But their opinions, along with those of other famous yachtsmen, have been influencing us to run in heavy weather using various methods—with warps, with bare poles, with storm sails.

In Allen Villers's book *The War with Cape Horn,* he tells of sailing the grain ship *Parma* from Australia, west to east around the Horn. In the roaring forties they were running with little sail set and were suddenly swept by a large wave, suffering extensive damage. The captain was the famous Ruben de Clouix. He hove the ship to and *Parma* suffered no more.

Captain Voss, another master sailor, has recommended heaving-to when heavy weather is encountered and gives details on how this can be done in vessels of all types and sizes in the appendix of his book *The Venturesome Voyage of Captain Voss*. This appendix is worth careful study and, in my opinion, should be carried for reference on board in every seagoing yacht.

Miles Smeeton notes in his section on heavy weather in his book *Because the Horn is There,* "I have been unable to find in Adlard Cole's book [*Heavy Weather Sailing*] any record of a yacht incurring damage while hove-to." We have hove-to on *Seraffyn*. I have lain hove-to in various boats while I was delivering them. Never once while lying hove-to have we suffered any damage.

I think we should reconsider the question of storm tactics and follow the example and advice of the master sailors instead of yachtsmen. We should listen to the men who spent up to nine months of every working year at sea, who often made thirty or forty trips around the Horn during their lifetimes, men who had experience on various types of sailing ships in all kinds of weather, men like Rueben de Clouix and Captain Voss.

To finish the quote that started this appendix, Voss says, **"So once more I repeat my advice: Be careful in running and heave-to rather a little earlier than deemed necessary by others."**

Heaving-To: The Sailor's Safety Valve

Heaving-to is a sailing tactic that buys you time: time to stop and rest, time to wait for the fog to clear, time for daylight to arrive so that you can enter a new port safely, time to double-check your navigation or do repairs. You can heave-to and wait near another ship while you transfer people or supplies. You can heave-to in rough-sea conditions to make it easier to take an important sight or bearing. Finally, when everything goes wrong and you are caught 100 miles off a lee shore with breaking waves stopping you from beating off, you must heave-to and hold on to your sea room. So all sailors, even those who advocate running before a storm, should know how to heave-to and be prepared to do so.

"Hove-to" means your boat is no longer sailing forward. It is stopped and making leeway with its bow about 50 degrees from the wind. The most erroneous thing I have read about heaving-to is "Simply back the staysail and set a reefed main." This does work on some boats in some conditions. But in strong winds with heavy seas, the bow on most boats will be forced off by the backed staysail, and the boat will usually end up slowly sailing along the trough of the waves. If the boat is making headway, you are not hove-to, you are sailing!

Since all sail plans have a different fore-and-aft balance and all hulls have a different center of lateral resistance, you must experiment with your own boat and find out how to hold its bow into the wind. Practicing in moderate to heavy winds and seas will give you an educated guess as to what to expect in stronger storm conditions. I have lain hove-to quite happily in our cutter with reefed mainsail only. Two of the ketches we delivered lay hove-to in Force 10 winds with just their mizzens sheeted in flat. Some fin and skeg boats heave-to with a storm jib on the backstay; others are happy with a storm trysail set; still others need a sea anchor or drogue to hold their bow up near the wind. Experimenting will teach you more about your hull and sail balance and will make your voyaging safer, more comfortable, and therefore more enjoyable.

Heaving-to in light to medium winds (up to 25 knots) is easily done by trimming your rudder and sails so that your boat is headed into the wind and sea as though you were close-hauled. Diagram A shows how *Seraffyn* heaves to with a full mainsail and the helm tied to leeward about 10 or 15 degrees. In the gusts, the mainsail luffs a bit but still does not have enough power to tack the boat through the eye of the wind. This is the stall point you want to achieve to heave-to correctly. In light to medium winds it is not vital to have the bow of the boat headed close to the wind, but your motion through the water should be stopped. Preventing this forward motion becomes very

Diagram A

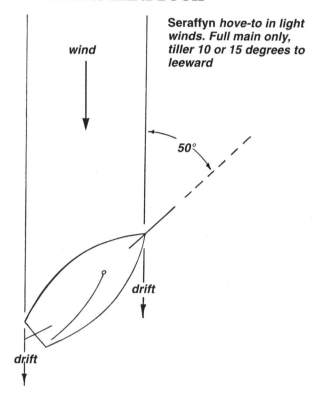

wind

Seraffyn *hove-to in light winds. Full main only, tiller 10 or 15 degrees to leeward*

50°

drift

drift

important when you are hove-to in breaking seas, as we will discuss later. A boat with a long keel and moderately cut-away forefoot would probably be able to heave-to as shown in **Diagram A**. Tie the tiller so that the boat will stall before it tacks. Some fin and skeg sloops are so lively that they will tack in the lightest winds if you set just the full main-sail. To combat this, try a reef in the main, adjust the helm more amid-ships, or back a staysail or small jib as shown in **Diagram B**.

Diagram C shows a ketch hove-to with the mizzen and reefed mainsail set. In lighter winds, ketches, with their sail area farther aft, will usually lie stopped with their bow 80 or 90 degrees to the wind. But as the wind increases they will begin to point closer to the hove-to position.

No matter what type of boat you are trying to get to lie hove-to, be sure to adjust your tiller at least a bit to leeward. If the tiller is tied to weather at all, an increase in wind strength could bear the boat off and cause her to gybe accidentally. Tie your tiller with heavy shock cord so that the cord absorbs some of the stress that would otherwise be exerted on the rudder assembly. Furthermore, for long-term cruis-ing safety, have rudder stops or lines to limit the distance your rudder can swing.

Heaving-to in heavy winds (gale to storm force), when the seas

Diagram B

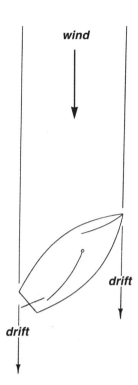

wind

drift

drift

Fin and skeg sloop with full main and small jib backed (sheeted to weather) in moderate winds. The tiller is adjusted so the boat stalls but does not tack. I dislike this method because the headsail sheet chafes against the weather shrouds

start to build, differs from heaving-to in moderate winds, because this is a tactic that uses the wake or slick of your boat to confuse the breaking seas. The key to heaving-to in these conditions is to get your boat to make a square drift, 90 degrees to the waves. This way you stay directly behind your amazingly protective slick. We lay hove-to in *Seraffyn* 400 miles east of England for 30 hours in a full Force 10 storm (50 to 55 knots of wind). Storm-force winds were reported in all European sea areas, from Iceland to northern Spain. By the second day the waves had built until they had long, overhanging crests, which were breaking dangerously on either side of our slick. Yet in the afternoon our foredeck was only damp from spray; the side decks had actually dried off in the September sun. No green seas had broken against our hull. Occasionally, broken-down white foam would skid across the slick to slap ineffectively against the bow. We'd lost only about 20 miles of the weathering we'd worked for two weeks to gain. I think this particular incident convinced Lin and me that as long as we had sea room, we could weather almost any storm we'd meet if we chose our sailing seasons carefully. When things did get rough, we could simply heave-to and feel as if we'd pulled over to the side of the road and parked.

Diagram D shows the method we used to hold *Seraffyn* hove-to in those storm-generated seas. Your boat may require different sail

Diagram C

wind

*Ketch hove-to in
moderate winds with
mizzen and reefed main*

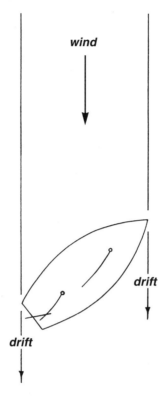

drift

drift

or helm adjustments. The most important factor is to make sure your boat is stopped and drifting downwind behind its slick. If you find you are forereaching, try tying the tiller more to leeward. The force of the wave action on the angled rudder pushes the stern of your boat down, the bow up. That is why tying the tiller to leeward helps stop the forward motion of your boat. In the same wind and sea conditions, a fin and skeg sloop might need a small sail set on the backstay (what could best be called a back-staysail). If this doesn't work, try a para-anchor with a back-staysail to keep your boat behind its slick.

Once we have any boat we are on properly hove-to, we usually hit the bunk. If we are in a fog or concerned about ships, we leave a strobe light flashing at the masthead. One of us goes on deck every hour to check for chafe on any storm gear. We check the set of the riding sail. Most important, we watch to see if the boat is forereaching. If your boat moves forward from behind your slick, a large sea could break onto your bow. To be sure we are not forereaching I have wet a couple of paper towels and dropped them into our slick. If the boat is staying directly to leeward of the slick, the paper towels will drift dead upwind. If the towels end up farther and farther aft of the boat, it means the boat is sailing forward out of its protection. You can see these white pieces of paper quite easily at night with a flashlight.

Diagram D

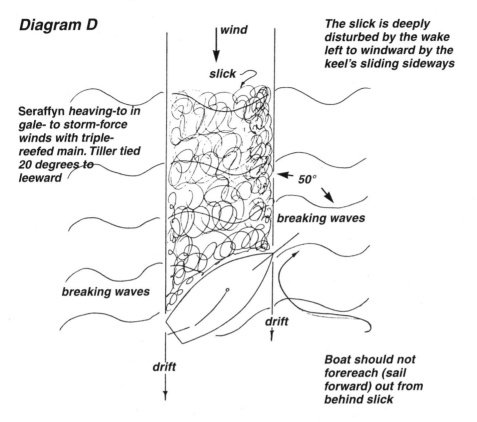

wind

The slick is deeply
disturbed by the wake
left to windward by the
keel's sliding sideways

slick

Seraffyn *heaving-to in
gale- to storm-force
winds with triple-
reefed main. Tiller tied
20 degrees to
leeward*

50°

breaking waves

breaking waves

drift

drift

Boat should not
forereach (sail
forward) out from
behind slick

If your boat is determined to forereach, you should set a sea anchor of some sort. Although there are a variety of sea anchors available, we prefer a para-anchor **(Photos 1 and 2).** This large-diameter drogue will definitely stop any forward motion, so that you drift directly behind your protective slick.*

We used a para-anchor with a triple-reefed mainsail on *Seraffyn* in the Gulf of Papagayo and in the North Pacific during storms with winds reported to range from Force 9 to hurricane. This 8-foot-diameter, coarsely woven nylon para-anchor is much stronger and easier to stow than the smaller-diameter, traditional iron-hooped canvas-cone sea anchors described in the older cruising books. The nylon para-anchor used with a nylon rode is more elastic than its canvas-and-manila counterpart and absorbs the shock of the boat surging against the sea anchor. This gear helps a vessel lie hove-to safely 50 degrees off the wind, as shown in **Diagram E,** even after the winds increase beyond storm force.

The first time we hove-to with a para-anchor and triple-reefed

---

*Eric Hiscock talks of this slick in the revised edition of his book *Cruising Under Sail* (Adlard Coles Nautical, pp. 371-73). The appendix in *Venturesome Voyages of Captain Voss* discusses this also.

Photo 1

Seraffyn'*s 8-foot-diameter parachute anchor, we use the same size and type on Taleisin

mainsail, *Seraffyn* lay almost head-to-wind in the manner described in the book *Venturesome Voyages of Captain Voss*. We were continuously woken up when the mainsail luffed violently as the para-anchor jerked us head to wind. This was really hard on the sail and hard on our nerves. We also felt that this head-to-wind position could be the reason Captain Voss reported having various rudders damaged during storms. Rudder damage is likely when a large, cresting sea pushes a boat straight astern so that the rudder is slammed over to one side. Another complaint we had about this head-to-wind position is that our boat no longer created a wide, protective slick. We later figured out how to lie in a close-hauled position even with the para-anchor set. Our keel's dragging sideways provided the slick to break down the seas so that they would have less force on our hull, rudder, and para-anchor gear. We rigged an adjustable fairlead, as shown in **Diagram F,** using gear we already had on board. This fairlead let us control the direction

Photo 2

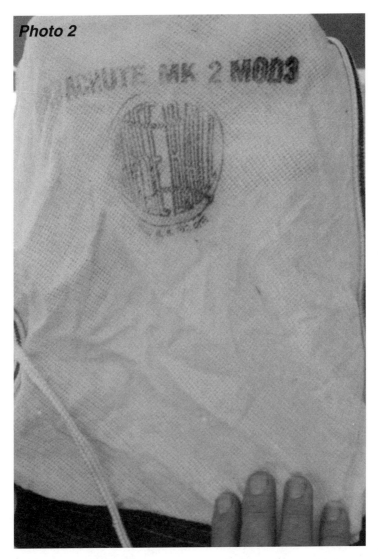

Close-up view shows the porous weave and strong construction of this parachute. This is a chute designed to pull ordnance out of aircraft and take the initial jerking load until the main chute opens. "BOURD," written on the chute, refers to Bureau of Ordnance

of the para-anchor strains in relation to the direction of the wind. Now we could lie 50 degrees off the wind. If any wave did sneak into our slick area, its force would first be exerted on the boat's bow. The bow would fall off to leeward, stretching and tugging on the nylon rode and para-anchor. They would absorb most of the shock so that the rudder received very little strain. This hove-to-with-para-anchor position also has another advantage. You are now presenting the corners of your

Diagram E

Seraffyn *hove-to with triple-reefed main and 8-foot-diameter para-anchor. This para-anchor is made of coarse-weave nylon stretchable fabric, which lets the water sieve through under strain. Both the boat and the para-anchor should be on the wave crests at the same time*

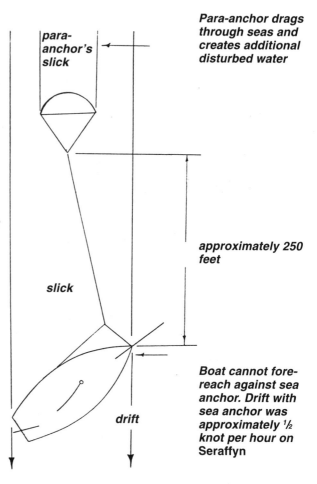

Para-anchor drags through seas and creates additional disturbed water

para-anchor's slick

approximately 250 feet

slick

Boat cannot fore-reach against sea anchor. Drift with sea anchor was approximately ½ knot per hour on Seraffyn

drift

cabins and hatches to the force of the sea **(Diagram G).** These corners are much stronger than the flat side or front of your cabin. Some people have hove-to stern to the wind and sea. This is less safe, because your relatively weak cockpit, sliding hatch, and companionway doors or drop boards are then vulnerable to a breaking sea.

Once you are lying-to the para-anchor you must adjust the length of the rode so that the boat and anchor are cresting their individual wave at the same time. If the boat is cresting one wave while the para-anchor is in the trough of another, the differences in the wave forces will cause an uncomfortable, gear-straining jerk.

One of the most important uses of a para-anchor is to cut your rate of drift. A boat running toward a lee shore, even if it is trailing warps, will be losing valuable sea room at the rate of 3 knots or more. A boat lying hove-to will lose about a knot, possibly less. *Seraffyn* lost an average of 5/8 of a knot during all of the times we lay hove-to without a para-anchor. A 54-foot centerboard ketch we delivered lost about

STORM MANAGEMENT

Diagram F

Pennant line from aft sheet winch to snatch block

Para-anchor line led to anchor windlass

The pennant line is secured to a normal-sized snatch block. The block rides on the main line. There is little chafe here, but be careful to protect the pennant line where it attaches to the snatch block (use a thimble or double turn) and also where it leads through or over the toerail

An oversized swivel snatch block works well here. We use a 4"-diameter sheave block with needle bearings on Taleisin ($^5/_8$" rode). The block must be well secured to take side loads; chafe can be great here

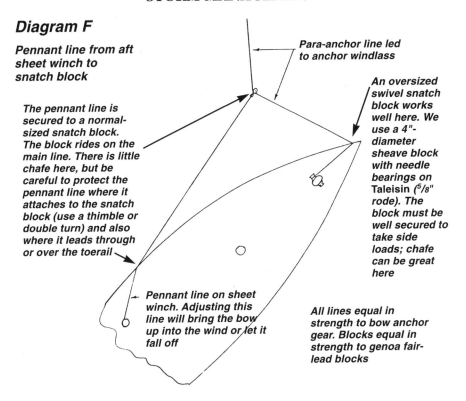

Pennant line on sheet winch. Adjusting this line will bring the bow up into the wind or let it fall off

All lines equal in strength to bow anchor gear. Blocks equal in strength to genoa fair-lead blocks

a knot each hour while we lay hove-to with the board down but no para-anchor set during a 52-hour, 50-knot blow in the Gulf of Mexico. When we set *Seraffyn*'s 8-foot-diameter para-anchor, our sights showed that our drift was cut to less than half a knot per hour.

The first time I set our para-anchor, I used the trip line and attached a long line from it all the way back to the boat. The para-anchor twisted on its connecting swivel and wound the trip line and anchor up like spaghetti. After this experience we eliminated the whole trip line. Although this slowed up the process of retrieving the sea anchor, it was still not too difficult. When it was safe to get under way again we used our anchor windlass to grind in the rode. As the boat and para-anchor lay in the trough of their waves, it was quite easy to winch in 6 or 8 feet of line. As the boat reached the crest of the wave, the line tension increased, so that we'd hold on and wait for the next trough. When the para-anchor was next to the bow, we hooked its edge with a boat hook and pulled it on board.

Setting the para-anchor was even easier than retrieving it. We laid it out on the foredeck to make sure none of its lines were tangled, shackled the second anchor rode* (a 300-foot-long, 5/8-inch three-

---

*This line is always ready to use. It is flaked into a separate section of the chain locker. The bitter end is secured belowdecks, with a round turn and two half-hitches. The outboard (anchor) end is hooked to the port chain pipe cap. To pull it out you simply lift the cap.

Diagram G

Sharp corners of deck structures are presented to the seas

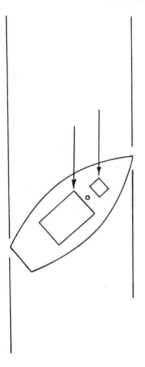

strand nylon line).* To the 3/8-inch galvanized swivel that is stored ready to use, attached to the para-anchor, then fed the para-anchor slowly over the bow, crown first. I eased out the line as the boat drifted slowly downwind. As soon as the rode was snubbed, the para-anchor filled and started working. It did not need any weights; it always opened as soon as the strains came on it.

Seraffyn's nylon para-anchor was not affected by mildew or rot. We did dry it out before we stowed it away each time. We also greased the galvanized swivel to keep it from rusting. After eleven years the para-anchor showed no signs of deterioration.

A question we are frequently asked is "How do you know it is time to stop and heave-to?" When we are beating, the decision is usually made for us. Waves start breaking against the weather bow and progress becomes extremely uncomfortable. Most cruising folks will stop going to windward about this same time, but racers quite often press on even after the seas are breaking dangerously.

To heave-to from a beating position, you simply drop your headsail and adjust the sails and helm to hold your boat in the close-hauled position, making a square drift to the seas. Once the boat is lying comfortably, I like to set up the main topping lift to take some of the strain off the leech of the reefed sail.

If we are beam-reaching, we heave-to before the waves break

STORM MANAGEMENT

Diagram H

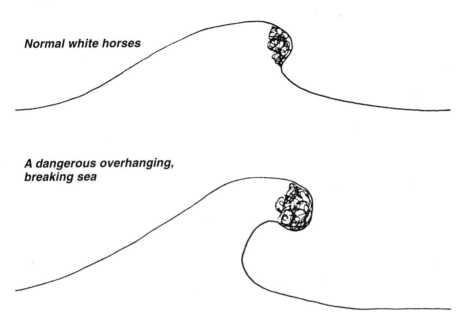

Normal white horses

A dangerous overhanging, breaking sea

hard against the hull. We'll often heave-to earlier on a beam reach than we do on a beat, because the flat side of our cabin, the port lights, and dinghy (which is stored on the cabin top) are particularly vulnerable to seas breaking on the beam. To heave-to from a beam reach, drop your headsail and sheet in your main, mizzen, or trysail as you round up on the back side of a wave. Try to choose a time when you will not hit the next breaking wave before the boat is stopped.

Choosing when it is time to heave-to is more difficult when you are running. We usually don't like to heave-to then, because we are making great time toward our goal. Running with the wind and seas also gives us a false sense of security. The decks are quite often dry; the waves are not slamming against the hull; the motion is usually more comfortable. So our rule is "heave-to before the waves start to over-hang," as in **Diagram H**. This is often hard to judge, but you'll realize it's time to heave-to when a sea breaks right under your stern and the boat is given an uneasy push. In other words, the power of the seas is starting to control the boat's normal progress through the water. Do not confuse this with ordinary surfing or acceleration down the face of a wave. If the boat is steering well, this is great fun. But as the seas get larger and more overhanging, your chances of broaching increase. Remember, the decision as to when it is time to heave-to depends completely on the shape of the wave, not on the speed of the wind. Theoretically, you could run under bare poles in winds of a hundred knots

Diagram I

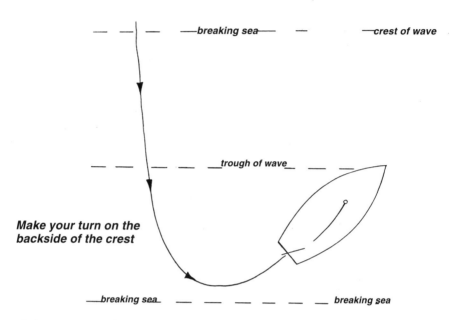

wind

—breaking sea— — —crest of wave

__trough of wave__ — —

Make your turn on the backside of the crest

__breaking sea__ — — — — — — breaking sea

if the sea were flat. On the other hand, in a rough situation such as is often found in the relatively shallow waters of the English Channel, where wind opposes tide and creates steep, breaking seas, running in Force 7 winds could be dangerous. So the classic rule is "heave-to as soon as you think about it." A falling barometer, wind clouds, and a tired crew will confirm your decision to heave-to early. Be prudent; the longer you wait to round up into those overhanging waves, the more fearsome and dangerous it will become.

When you decide to stop running, drop your headsail, sheet in your reefed mainsail, mizzen, or trysail, and round quite quickly into the wind. You'll probably take on a good bit of spray as you round through the beam-reaching position. The boat will heel sharply, but there is no danger if you decide to heave-to before breaking waves make the boat feel uneasy **(Diagram I)**.

Once you are hove-to and have the boat settled down, study the size and power of the breaking waves. When you are lying hove-to, it is a real temptation to start sailing before it is safe. You seem too comfortable, thanks to the calming effect of your slick and the relaxed feel of your boat now that it is no longer thrusting through the water. So you are sometimes lulled into a false sense of security. Be positive that the waves have decreased in size and power before you start sailing again.

It is my firm belief that heaving-to has become an unused art,

Diagram J

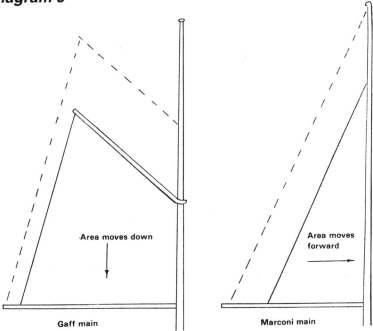

Area moves down

Area moves forward

Gaff main

Marconi main

because most modern yacht designs are for racer-cruiser-type hulls, which usually do not track as well or lie as still as older, long-keeled boats. Added to this is the fact that many of those older boats were gaff rigged. Their sail plans did not move forward when they were reefed, as sail plans do on modern Marconi rigs **(Diagram J)**. This sail area well aft helped hold the bow up into the wind; their long keels held them steady so that they hove-to quietly and easily, with no fussing with back-staysails, drogues, or sea anchors—just drop the jib, sheet in the main-sail, and relax. Also, the older generation of sailors worked all year round. Fishing boats hove-to while they pulled their nets; pilot cutters hove-to and waited for ships; square riggers hove-to to wait for the fog to clear before they closed the land. Weather was no deterrent. Those working sailors had to be out there. The British navy blockaded the French coast winter and summer, year in, year out, in all sizes of sail-ing vessels, from three-deckers down to 40-foot dispatch cutters. It was vital that these sailors knew how to heave-to when gales and fog fanned across the English Channel and into the Bay of Biscay. Today's yachts-men who are sailing for pleasure can organize their races or holiday cruises to coincide with the most favorable weather and wind condi-tions. The same is true of those who sail around the world west-about with the prevailing winds. These people can choose to sail when con-ditions are most favorable, when gales and storms of long duration are rare, so that seas don't have time to build up dangerously.

But even with the best of planning, there will be times when you need to know how to heave-to. Although boats have changed, sailors have not. They still get tired and need rest. Modern boats can be made to heave-to, but since they don't balance the same way as their working ancestors, try experimenting with a sail on the backstay, sheeted-in mizzens, trysails, and para-anchors, so that you can take advantage of the sailor's safety valve.

Gale and Storm Incidents

The following excerpts from our cruising books show how our storm tactics worked on 24-foot, 7-inch *Seraffyn*. They also record our feelings about some of the strongest winds we faced those first eleven years of our cruising life.

From *Cruising in* Seraffyn

We had celebrated our escape from heavy weather in the Gulf of Tehuantepec too soon. As we crossed the Gulf of Papagayo, strong winds hit us dead on the nose. We were sailing along when we saw a squall approaching. Before we had the genoa completely down, it was blowing a gale. We reefed the main and waited for the squall to end; it didn't. Under staysail and double-reefed main, we beat toward Punta Giones, 300 miles ahead. The first night, we decided to heave-to — mainsail double-reefed and tiller lashed slightly alee. Looming seas roared toward us, but *Seraffyn's* bowsprit lifted bravely to each one, and in the morning the foredeck was dry.

At dawn on the second day, the wind moderated and we set our staysail again. After Larry shot the sun, we found our noon-to-noon run was a poor 36 miles. As night fell, the wind picked up again. We decided to try our sea anchor. *Seraffyn* would heave-to happily without it, but someday, we felt, we might have to use the sea anchor in an extreme storm, or when we had limited sea room, and this was a good time to test it.

With the main double-reefed, as soon as the 8-foot-diameter parachute filled with water, it pulled *Seraffyn's* head directly into the wind with a jerk, but within a few minutes we felt the sea anchor becoming less and less effective. We winched it in to find it had wound itself around the trip line, collapsing the chute. We removed the trip line and set the anchor again; this time it worked fine. The parachute tried to hold us head to wind, but allowed our bow to fall off on either tack about 40 degrees. During the night the motion became irritating, because the main slatted furiously through the eye of the wind every 10 minutes or so. Still, we seemed secure. In the morning the wind had moderated, and we hauled in the sea anchor. As we crested each wave, the sea anchor line would slacken a bit and we could winch it in about 6 feet. When the sea anchor was finally under the bow, Larry grabbed the lines on one side of it and spilled out the water. Then he heaved it on deck and stowed it. Without the trip line, the swivel had worked well, the rope hadn't kinked and the lines didn't scramble.

We set sail again, our log showing a noon-to-noon run of 60 miles, while our noon sight put us one mile astern of our previous noon's fix! What a disappointment. When our regular nightly wind increase arrived, we decided to heave-to under reefed mainsail. This produced a much easier motion than the night before, when we were riding to the sea anchor. "Next time we use the sea anchor," Larry said, "I'd like to try leading the warp from a point about halfway between the chainplates and the stemhead. That way I think she will lie-to on one tack instead of changing over, and causing all that annoying motion down below. Besides that, lying about 45 degrees to the wind should take some of the strain off the rudder fittings, the rudder, and the sea-anchor cable."

North Atlantic Crossing

In the morning the wind blew from the north. With our usual optimism we set a full mainsail, staysail, and lapper. All through that day we reached along with the wind growing slowly and with us tying in one reef after another. By morning we had covered 119 miles, and we were down to staysail only. The radio from Cape Finisterre, Spain, reported north winds, Force 10. *Seraffyn* slammed into the seas, heeling to the gusts. Life below became miserable.

"I'm going to heave her to, Lin," Larry said. "You stay below. No sense in both of us getting wet."

Larry uncleated the staysail sheet and handed it to me through the companionway. "Let it go when I yell," he said. I listened to the howl of the wind in the rigging, the sound of breaking, rushing seas and spray. I heard Larry yell and let go of the sheet.

Snap! Crack! The flogging staysail shook the boat from stem to stern, banging like a cannon gone mad. I froze, and my mind went blank with fear. Tears rushed to my eyes as *Seraffyn* rolled sailless in the trough of crashing seas.

The noise diminished when Larry hoisted the triple-reefed main which pointed *Seraffyn* into the wind, and tied the tiller slightly alee. I mentally caught ahold of myself as our motion ceased and the noise died away.

Larry came below and found me crying. "What's wrong?" he asked. I managed a smile. "The noise scared me," I said.

The motion hove-to, as always, was wonderful. Maybe it's just the contrast but it feels like sudden peace after a long war. Instead of a one-pot meal, I made a dinner of an onion omelet, boiled potatoes, and a tossed cabbage salad. After dinner we played cribbage and listened to English weather reports: "Force 10 winds for all sea areas."

STORM MANAGEMENT

Larry went on deck to check the oil lamps while I washed the dishes. Before I climbed into the snug quarterberth, I checked to make sure all the pans were secure in their racks. No noise from loose galley ware, no rattles from on deck. Larry came below, and all was well in our world, although the wind shrieked through the rigging.

We lay hove-to for 30 hours, and then finally the wind eased and we set our staysail to match the triple-reefed main. We were now within the area covered by the BBC's weather reports, and their predictions of Force 4 northerly winds were accurate.

The sun was peeking over the horizon the next morning when I went on deck to look around. "Why didn't you tell me there was a yacht out here?" I called down to Larry.

Larry grumbled, "Let me sleep. I don't want to hear any more fantasies."

"Don't believe me," I retorted, hardening the sheets and resetting Helmer to work toward the schooner. That maneuver convinced Larry. He came on deck and looked at the tiny mound of canvas off to windward of us. "Set the staysail, Lin," he said.

We raced *Seraffyn* over the calm seas, carrying all the canvas she could take. People! Another yacht crazy enough to be 300 miles from land! We drew closer, and Larry went below to sleep again. By noon we had caught the 49-foot schooner. Her crew were just as anxious to talk as we were. We slid alongside, 30 feet off their rail, and dropped our staysail to keep pace with them.

"Where are you coming from?" I yelled, noting as we came up to her that she was the *Wilhelm.*

"San Miguel, Azores, 20 days out!" a crewman called.

"We're out of Horta, 16 days," I called.

"We're almost out of stores,"one man yelled. "No cigarettes, no booze."

Throw us a line," Larry shouted. The man tied a sailbag to a line and heaved it, as both boats reached along at 4 knots. Larry put a bottle of rum in the bag and tossed it back into the water. The four men on *Wilhelm* cheered as they took it out of the bag—and each took a slug straight from the bottle.

"Hell of a storm," the man at the wheel yelled. "We were almost to England when it blew up. We lost 200 miles running before it."

We had lost only 18 miles lying hove-to in the same storm.

From Seraffyn's *European Adventure:* Broach

The equinoctial gales our sailing friends from Sweden, Finland, and Poland had warned us about proved to be no myth. By September 18, 1973, the morning after we tied up in Bornholm's Ronne harbor, an easterly storm was blowing. *Seraffyn* lay comfortably in the corner of the fish haven, completely surrounded by almost a hundred Danish fishing trawlers. The wind moaned through the forest of rigging surrounding us, and rain hurled down in sheets. For five days the wind blew at gale force with gusts to 70 knots.

At first we welcomed the enforced stay in port. I had mending to do. Larry was busy writing and reading. The local library had a large collection of English-language magazines. But we grew restless after our mail packet arrived at the local post office and we finished answering every letter in it.

"We're only about 160 miles from Thruro," I told Larry one evening after we'd returned from a walk decked out in full wet-weather gear plus three sweaters each. "Three good days' sailing and we'll be where we want to spend the winter."

Larry looked over my shoulder to study the chart of the natural harbor in front of Walstead's shipyard. "Looks good and safe, Lin. I'm sure we'll be able to take *Seraffyn* out of the water to revarnish her insides." We turned off the tiny butane heater we'd connected to one burner of our stove, then crawled into our Dacron-filled double sleeping bag. We quietly discussed the refit *Seraffyn* needed, now that she was almost five years old. One or the other of us kept thinking of new items to add to our growing work list until we fell asleep, cuddled warmly together.

Each day the fisherman who owned the boats around us would come down from their homes in town to check their mooring lines, start their engines, and exchange news with their friends. One or the other would translate the latest weather forecast for us. On the sixth day the sky was clear and the wind did seem lighter when we opened our hatch in the early morning. By 1000 the wind was definitely lighter. The owner of the small steel yacht tied near us called, "Come listen to the forecast." He translated as a German announcer said, "Wind easterly, Force 6 to 7, decreasing to 4 or 5."

All around us the trawlers started to come to life. Their crews arrived from town shouting merrily across the water. A hundred fishing boats maneuvered out of the inner harbor, one after another. By noon there was only one trawler, the steel yacht, and ourselves left in the south end of the previously crowded harbor. "I'm not sure I want to go," I said, tapping the barometer that stood good and high at almost 1015 millibars. It didn't move. The flag on the harbormaster's office had stopped whipping and just waved gaily in the slightly gusty Force 5 east wind. Larry seemed reluctant, too. "It's dead downwind from here. Since it's about 85 miles to the light at Klintholm, we could leave as late as 1400 and still be sure of arriving during daylight. Let's wait another three or four hours. If the wind continues to drop, we'll set off."

I cooked up a pot of stew while I made lunch, figuring that it would be wise to have dinner ready in case the leftover seas outside were rough. At 1230 the people on the steel yacht prepared to sail. The four young Germans on board the 30-foot *Tummler* had to get home to their jobs in Kiel. But still we were reluctant to cast off our mooring lines, although neither of us could put a finger on what was bothering us. At 1300 the last trawlermen cast off their lines and headed out onto the steadily calming sea. At 1400 neither of us could think of any logical excuses to stay in the harbor. We maneuvered *Seraffyn* around until she was pointing bow to the wind, then hoisted the double-reefed mainsail and staysail, cast off our doubled-up mooring lines, and reached into the center of the basin. As we tacked for the narrow entrance, the harbormaster came out of his office and called, "Good sailing." And it was good sailing, as we ran wing-and-wing out of Ronne Harbor. The sea was calm, protected by the mass of Bornholm Island. Our small sails pulled us at top speed. We decided to eat an early dinner and really enjoyed the stew. Dark seemed to come extra early that evening as the skies clouded over and the wind began to increase. Before I went below to climb into the bunk, I helped Larry drop the mainsail, furl it, and secure the boom in the gallows. We'd already put one drop board into the companionway even though there was no spray on deck. We'd made it a rule that as soon as there was a reef in the mainsail, a drop board belonged in place. Since the first of the drop boards has its top higher than the level of our deck, water that gets into the cockpit during heavy weather can't easily find its way below decks.

Larry put our handy canvas companionway cover in place over the rest of the opening because the ever-increasing wind was cold. I was undressed down to a long-sleeve-T-shirt, underpants, and socks when Larry pulled aside the canvas and said, "Hey, Bug, how about sleeping in my bunk tonight. It's on the windward side so if a bit of spray does come on board it won't get the sleeping bag wet." I was surprised at his suggestion, because I prefer sleeping against the hull on the leeward side of *Seraffyn* when there is any motion. But I switched the bag across and set the lee cloth in place. One oil lamp glowed softly above the galley, swinging gaily in its gimbals as we roared off the backs of the growing seas. I squirmed around until I could lift the canvas companionway cover. I saw Larry standing in back of the boom gallows, his elbows over the stout piece of teak on which the mainboom now rested, as we ran under just the staysail. Our oil-burning stern light bounced beside him, its light gleaming off his high black seaboots. He looked comfortable and warm enough in his sweater-bulged windbreaker and jeans. Our ship's bell rang four times, and I secured the lashing on the lee cloth, turned over, and went easily to sleep.

How can anyone describe the horrid sensation I felt when I was thrown halfway out of the bunk? Only the lee cloth kept me from going farther. *Seraffyn* made a huge whunking sound as she was hurled off the top of a breaking sea. The horrid crashing sound of flying cans, tools, books, floorboards, and dishes drowned out the rushing sound of the huge stream of water that pushed past the canvas companionway cover. We seemed to be upside down, then I was tossed just as violently back into the quarter berth. I struggled clear of the sleeping bag, sheet, and lee cloth in the solid darkness. I could only scream— "Larry, Larry! — then my feet hit the water that sloshed fore and aft as *Seraffyn* resumed her running motion. I was standing calf-deep in water grabbing for a flashlight when Larry yelled, "I'm here. Start pumping!" I found the bilge pump handle, inserted it in the pump, and started stroking. Floating floorboards hit my ankles, making watery-sounding thunks as they collided with the settee fronts. I had the water down three or four inches when Larry yelled, "Don't worry when the boat's motion changes." He poked his soaking-wet head past the canvas cover, "I'm going to head into the wind and heave-to. Everything's all right now, Bug."

I flashed the light around the horribly littered cabin, pumping all the while. All the books from our navigation shelf were in the sink. The lenses from two oil lamps lay in shattered pieces on the drainboard. Most of the tools from the locker in the starboard settee were now on top of the quarter berth. Had I been sleeping there I'd have been hit by chisels, woodplanes, screwdrivers, wrenches — over a hundred pounds of flying sharp metal. Something kept tapping my leg. When the beam of my light picked up my toothbrush floating merrily on top of the remaining fifty or sixty gallons of unwelcome ocean that had invaded my previously tidy home, I finally broke down and started crying.

Larry hoisted the double-reefed mainsail. *Seraffyn's* motion changed as she heeled to a gust of wind on her beam, then rounded into the wind, slowed down, and finally stopped, heeling about 15 degrees. She began to assume the comfortable, safe-feeling motion that I knew meant we were hove-to.

Larry climbed below just then. "Got to get an oil lamp burning fast. We're surrounded by fishing boats," he was saying as he took my flashlight and looked around. Then he noticed my tear-streaked face. He tugged off his dripping windbreaker, put his soggy-sweatered arms around me, and started rocking me, whispering, "It's all right now, baby, we're okay."

I realized that Larry was shivering in his wet clothes. My stockinged feet were still covered with sloshing water. "Get out of those wet clothes," I commanded, trying to catch hold of myself. I grabbed for a paper towel to wipe my tears only to get a handful of soggy paper from the towel roller. Larry took charge. "Find me some oil lamp lenses. Every one in our navigation lamps shattered when they filled with water." Our linen locker on the starboard side had stayed completely dry, so I handed Larry a fresh towel along with his new lenses. He first got a cabin light going. Then he finished pumping the bilges. "I'm sure glad we moved the bilge pump to a position inside the cabin," he commented as our Whale Gusher 10 made sucking and gurgling sounds.

The kind, golden light of two oil lamps made our mess look less frightening. Larry went back on deck, retrieved and lit our running lights, then finally stripped. When I rummaged in our clothes locker I found that over half of Larry's clothes were dry, but all of mine were soaked because they were on the lower shelf. I stripped too, then both of us dressed in Larry's dry warm sweaters and jeans, laughing just a bit at the luck that made me store Larry's clothes on the upper shelves of our locker. "Can you imagine me trying to get into one of your sweaters?" Larry teased. Then we started storing things somewhat back in place. A cup of hot chocolate laced with brandy tasted wonderful, and I finally convinced Larry to climb into the miraculously dry sleeping bag when he started to shiver again. "You'll have to keep a good watch on deck," Larry warned me. "there are still lots of fishing boats around, so be ready to ease the mainsheet and bear off to move clear if anything gets too close."

His shivering soon stopped and finally he told me the deckside version of our mishap. "After you went to sleep the wind increased a lot more. The seas were growing, probably because we were clear of Bornholm's lee. *Seraffyn* was going too fast even with just the staysail. I considered heaving-to, but there were all of those fish trawlers heading back toward the protection of the island. I figured it would be best to run past the last of them, then heave-to. So I dropped the staysail and reset Helmer to put the wind dead aft. *Seraffyn* kept running at about 3 knots under bare poles. Helmer held her perfectly on course. I was standing on the afterdeck, behind the boom gallows, holding on, watching that keen little steering vane do its work. There was just a low-flying spray hitting my seaboots. I didn't even once consider putting on wet gear. Then I looked astern and said to myself, 'That one is going to get me wet.' Well, the wave broke right over our stern. Next thing I knew, I was completely under, plastered against the boom gallows by a huge weight of water. Boy, did I hold on tight! I'll bet you can see fingerprints in the teak. Then my head came clear. All I could see was white foam all around, no boat at all. I can just remember thinking of you trapped below before I saw one tip of one spreader break clear of the foam. Then I knew she was going to come up. The mast leaped clear, and seconds later *Seraffyn* seemed to shake herself dry. The windvane took over and we were running downwind again as if nothing had happened. The amazing thing is, the vane itself was bent at least 30 degrees to port, yet it could still steer the boat. God, it all happened so fast! I should have hove-to and stayed on deck with our big flashlight. When I think about it now, those fishing boats would have seen us; they must have been watching, too."

Larry finally fell asleep. *Seraffyn* rode to the steadily howling storm, lying about 50 degrees off the wind. The wind and sea seemed to increase during the next three hours. Once a sea smashed against our bow, sending a heavy clatter of spray against the cabin front, but no green water came on deck. A heavy rain started, and by dawn the wind abated enough so that we felt safe in laying off toward the Swedish harbor of Ysted, 14 miles away on a reaching course. In the gray, rain-streaked dawn we could finally assess the damage we'd sustained. Our pride and joy, a 30-year-old copper and brass oil-lamp-lit binnacle with a 4-year-old, 4-inch Ritchie compass had disappeared from its wooden bracket. The 1-inch-diameter bronze pipe lifeline stanchion that we lashed the blade of our 14-foot oar to was bent at almost 45 degrees. The dinghy, lashed firmly to its chocks on the cabin top, had been loosened up, and closer inspection showed that one of the bronze brackets holding the chocks to the cabin top had been bent like a pretzel and its 2-inch, number 14 screws pulled loose from the oak framing of the cabin top. The inside of the cabin top was cracked from the force the dinghy had exerted. Inside, the damage was minimal: a lot of dented varnish work from flying tools, several broken bottles, loads of wet clothes, and five broken oil-lamp lenses. We were glad we'd had no engine because oil or fuel from the bilges would have made matters worse. Since the only electric equipment on board was the portable radio, which had been on the windward side and stayed completely dry, we were able to get all ship's systems working in short order despite the huge amount of water that had come on board. Every bit of the damage, both inside and on the deck, occurred on the port side of the boat, the side that fell into the trough of the wave.

We used our hand-bearing compass to steer by. Ysted came into view by 1000, although visibility was made poor by driving rain. We reached into its almost deserted yacht basin and sighed with relief as we tied our lines securely. I pulled all our wet clothes out onto the rain-soaked decks. Larry stuffed them into sailbags and we carted them into town. The lady at the laundromat was amazed at our soggy mass of clothes, so we explained what had happened. When we returned to the small harbor, we found that she had called the local newspaper—a reporter was waiting for us. "You know, a 400-ton coaster sank only 17 miles from here yesterday evening," he told us. Then he drove us to the main harbor to see the unhappy crew of a 200-ton coaster slowly moving a shattered cargo of roofing tiles to correct the 17-degree list their ship had assumed after being hit by a rogue wave the night before. They'd lost most of their deck cargo, and only made port with the assistance of a huge car ferry that had responded to their May Day call. The ferry had stayed carefully to windward of the coaster, giving them a lee for the 18-mile voyage into Ysted Harbor.

We began wondering about the 30-foot German yacht that had left Ronne an hour before us. And to this day we don't know what happened to *Tummler* and her crew of four. "You people should know better than to sail during the equinoctial gales," the reporter commented, echoing the warning we'd had from dozens of Baltic sailors. We'd ignored them all and paid the price.

Typhoon

Wonder if the shipping routes shown on our pilot chart are wrong," I asked Larry our fourth night out of Galle, Sri Lanka. "I was thinking the same thing," he answered. "I saw three ships on my last watch. How many did you count?"

I'd seen the lights of four freighters on the horizon to the north of us as we reached along on an easterly course.

We'd headed southeast for the first three days of this voyage; our goal: three degrees north latitude, the normal lower limit of the typhoon zone. When our log reading and DR track showed we'd reached this point, we changed course to head directly east for 600 miles before working northeast into the Andaman Sea. We'd had cloudy skies for two days, so when our first sight this fourth morning out made no sense, we waited anxiously for our noon sight, while we both went over Larry's navigation figures, trying to find some mistake in the arithmetic. The noon sight seemed so out of whack that we wanted to ignore it. "We couldn't possibly be 110 miles north of our course," was Larry's grumbled comment as he rechecked his figures and read the sextant again. Then I reminded him of the ships we'd seen. They should have been at least a hundred miles north of us. "If some sort of current was setting us north . . ."

"Can't be a two-and-a-half-knot current," Larry stated. "Pilot charts show a southeasterly current coming out of the Bay of Bengal at this time of the year!"

But our first afternoon sight made sense only if we accepted our noon sight. That started us worrying. "If something has caused a current that strong, it must be a pretty big disturbance," Larry said. "Let's get headed south again." We tightened our sheets until we were sailing on a close reach 45 degrees away from our rhumb-line course. Within a few hours the last ship dropped below the horizon astern of us. Then we got the second sign.

A long, slow swell began to interrupt the steady pattern of the seas that came rolling toward us. Along with the normal wind waves, this rolling surge added an awkward motion to our 5- knot charge into the sea. I got out our stopwatch and counted the seconds between each crest of these obviously different swells. Four swells passed each minute, instead of the normal eight or ten. Their unusually slow spacing began to add to our certainty. There was a big weather disturbance somewhere ahead of us! Then the barometer needle moved more than one millibar from the spot it seemed to have settled in over the past three weeks. Each hour it dropped another notch, moving slowly from 1008 to 1007 and down to 1000. Each drop was accompanied by another hint at the winds that lay somewhere ahead and slightly to the east of us. Fine mare's tails began to lace the sky above us, radiating from the east, causing the sun to glow yellow and milky. Then the humidity began to increase until we shed all of our clothes to try and be comfortable even during the night. The second day after we'd discovered the strange north-moving current, our winds began to get squally.

Two of our working sails, the main and lapper, were now over three years old. We'd had to patch a few holes already. The lower panels of the mainsail were pretty tender from the burning ultraviolet rays of the sun. In Sri Lanka we'd sent letters off to sailmakers in England and Hong Kong, asking for price quotes on new sails. Our plan was to have them built and shipped to us in Singapore for our April departure up the China Sea. So when our lapper developed a split 11 feet long just at the reef points, we weren't too shocked. But as Larry set to work taking a long line of herringbone stitches while I helped hold the fabric in place, this sail failure added to my apprehensions. We sat wedged against the dinghy on the cabin top, working on that sail for three hours as the ominous swell grew evermore apparent. Typhoon. The word loomed ever larger in my mind. I tried talking out my fears, but after two days of gradually increasing signs, of reading every word we could find in our limited shipboard library about tropical disturbances and the best way to handle them, there just wasn't anything left to say. "The boat's as ready as she'll ever be. From the information we have now, we're on the right tack. If we keep trying to get south and east, it's the best we can do," Larry said, as we finished patching the aging sail. "I've got the sea anchor where I can get at it easily. You've got bread and fruit ready in case you can't cook up anything else. It might pay to make some soup up after dinner, just to have something extra. Other than that, it's just wait and see. Might already be past us."

By the time the lapper was patched, our wind had steadied at 20 knots from the east-northeast, so we stowed the sail below and continued romping on with our staysail and single reefed main as dark settled in.

Then the mare's tails thickened into rolls of gray cumulus. I'd seen clouds like these one time before. They'd crept over us as we lay at anchor in the Chesapeake Bay and we got whipped by Hurricane Agnes. So I anxiously tapped the barometer while Larry trimmed and lit the oil lamps. The needle steadied at 999 millibars. Not very low, when I considered the barometer readings we'd had in the Chesapeake. That time we'd had pressures as low as 987.

"You've got to stop worrying this storm in," Larry said through a mouthful of fish cakes. "Best thing you can do is get some sleep. If you're well rested, you'll be far better off if something does hit us." So I climbed into the bunk and, in spite of the stuffy heat in the closed-up cabin, did fall asleep. When Larry shook me awake three hours later, the motion was a bit rougher. "I've put in another reef. Squalls and lightning to the north of us," Larry said, as he had a small shot of rum.

STORM MANAGEMENT

"Everything seems fine, winds up, maybe 30 knots. Barometer hasn't moved. Maybe we'll miss the worst of it."

I climbed out from between the cotton sheets and took a look around on deck. Even the occasional light spray that hit my bare body felt warm in the sultry, wind-pushed air. Thunder rumbled in the distance; lightning hidden by the clouds lit the sky ahead and north of us like flashbulbs behind a shaded window.

I went below and pulled out our tattered copy of Bowditch* and again read, "The passage of a tropical cyclone at sea is an experience not soon to be forgotten." An hour later, that sentence came rushing through my wind-whipped mind.

I'd watched the squall line creep closer, its majestic clouds outlined by lightning, its movement orchestrated by thunder. Nothing else seemed to change. The swell ran at the same 10- or 12-foot height; the wind waves crashed just forward of our beam. *Seraffyn* drove through the seas at 5 knots; her motion, if not steady, was at least predictable. Then a separate jarring crash of lightning illuminated my whole world in eerie gray and white. I could see the creeping foot of a granddaddy squall only 300 yards to windward, pouring rain forming a ruffled skirt over its froth-white toes. I charged below and grabbed my wet-weather jacket, then climbed out into the cockpit as fast as I could. I barely had that plastic-coated parka on when the first gust hit. *Seraffyn* staggered until her cabin side kissed the rushing waves. I slid to the leeward side of the cockpit, threw loose the staysail sheet, and let the sail flog. *Seraffyn* steadied, and I crawled forward to drop the staysail before it ripped itself to bits. Driving rain hit at me; spray flew across the foredeck. I didn't need a light; flashes of lightning were almost continuous now. When I bent to lash the staysail down to the bowsprit and windlass, wind-driven rain and spray stung at my bare rear end like buckshot. Tears or saltwater filled my eyes—I'll never know which—and I kept thinking, "I should go get Larry . . . I'd better slow *Seraffyn* down some more . . . ." But I just kept working, remembering the times I'd helped Larry settle the boat into a hove-to position. I put two extra lashings under the bowsprit and around the staysail just to be sure it would stay put. I crawled aft and starting hauling in the mainsheet. That's when Larry came into the cockpit decked out in foul-weather gear. "Did you unclutch the wind vane?" he yelled directly into my ear. I shook my head no, and he began doing the things I usually did while I remembered each detail of the jobs Larry handled when we lay *Seraffyn* hove-to to face the howling wind. I grabbed one of the cockpit flotation cushions and lashed it to the taffrail knee, where it would act as a shock absorber for the tiller. Then I lashed the tiller 20 degrees to leeward against the cushion. *Seraffyn* heeled but soon stopped moving forward. I climbed up the rain-slicked deck to look at the wake she was making on her windward side. A smoothed-out patch of water

*See appendix, page 143

began to form, disturbed by her long keel. Now we were making no headway at all, just drifting slowly, dead downwind, the bow pointed about 50 degrees off the wind. Waves broke forward off the bow and astern of us, but when they hit that protective slick, they seemed to crumble, then turned to powerless foam. So I checked over the deck as Larry unlashed, then removed the wind vane's Dacron cover.

It's amazing how much calmer everything seemed with the boat settled down, the halyards tied off, the vibration of that 6-square-foot vane quieted down. *Seraffyn* seemed to ride like a duck over the building seas. Lashing rain smashed the wave crests so that they were too flat to break, but nothing muffled the sound of the constant thunder.

When Larry came close and yelled, "I'll take one last look around. You get below before you catch pneumonia," I gladly climbed into the comparative quiet of the cabin. As soon as Larry came in, he shed his dripping foul-weather gear and began toweling down my legs and back. That's when he noticed the red dots all over my thighs and bottom. He collapsed into roars of laughter, then dug out a mirror so I could see the bruises the driving spray had left. We needed that break in the tension. Neither of us wanted to say the word typhoon. But when I was wrapped up in a blanket and slowly warming in the bunk, Larry drew a rough sketch of the typical typhoon wind pattern and reasoned, "We're definitely on the safe semicircle. The winds and our drift will shove us away from the center. Nothing more we can do but hope our mainsail holds. If it doesn't, I'll get the sea anchor out."

For the next eight hours the wind shrieked and howled through our rigging. Seas grumbled and washed along our leeward deck each time a swell passed under us. The lightning and thunder would have kept us awake if the increasingly rough motion hadn't been enough. How hard did it blow? Far over gale force was all we could guess. How high were the seas? Not as big as we'd seen them in the north Atlantic, when we lay hove-to for 30 hours with full storm warnings in all sea areas. But the wind and sea were irregular, puffing, changing direction, unstable. Through it all *Seraffyn* rode lightly, her tightly sheeted double-reefed main trying to drive her up into the wind, her lashed-down tiller working to keep her there. She made almost no headway, giving easily to each sea that crested against her bow. We rarely heard anything more than heavy spray hit the deck. Her drift seemed to be about three-quarters of a knot dead downwind. I remember saying at some time during that long night, "The reality is easier to take than the two days of anticipation."

Larry agreed, but later, while we lay in the quarter berths opposite each other, bracing to the lurch-and-lunge motion, he suddenly thought out loud, "What about *Crusader*? If Don didn't take any sights, that current would have set him way north and he'd never have known about it. That could have put him on the wrong side of this typhoon." I considered this for a while, remembering *Crusader's* leaking hull, her large windows and rotten spreaders. Then I dismissed it all. "They left two days ahead of us. *Crusader* powers at 6 knots. Probably almost in Thailand by this time."

Daylight slowly crept into the closed boat; occasional patches of blue sky passed the salt-stained port lights. Our double-faced compass showed that the wind had shifted more to the west; our barometer was up two millibars. But now the seas seemed worse, more confused. Larry got on his wet gear, took out two drop boards, and climbed into the cockpit for a look around. The oil lamps were miraculously still burning, giving us even more faith in their rebuilt burners. *Seraffyn* seemed to be forereaching just a bit, maybe because the wind was gusty now, and a bit lighter. She was definitely moving out of the slick her keel made, so Larry yanked on the mainsheet to try and get it in even flatter. That did it. Our tired old sail split. I heard it go and felt the boat's motion change. Now she rolled between each lunge. "Get ready," Larry called down the companionway, "I'm bringing the mainsail down below. Get me a screwdriver." I struggled into the tool locker, with lack of sleep, the rough motion, and a new set of worries putting me on the edge of seasickness.

Larry brought in good news with the unruly mass of shredded sail. "Sea's going down fast. Still blowing close to a gale, but there's a line of blue sky ahead. I think we can lie ahull safely. Let's get this sail fixed."

I was fine as we worked together drying the torn part of the sail with towels, then piecing the two halves together. I held the edges of the 11-foot tear roughly in place while Larry took huge herringbone stitches with waxed Dacron thread. In the worst places we used duct tape to hold the sail temporarily together. I prayed we were matching the two halves somewhat closely, because we could spread only 3 feet at a time in the sail-filled cabin. Then Larry did it. He opened the 1-quart can of contact cement and started gluing a three-inch wide strip of Dacron over our stitching. One whiff and I was out the companionway and in the lee scuppers; the hell with foul-weather gear. I lay in the fresh air watching Larry work and mentally awarding him a hero badge as he gooped that smelly glue over the patch, patiently waiting for it to dry, then lined the now self-stick strip over the stitches. But I had my consolation as I watched the sun creep over us and the seas slowly start to take on a more normal pattern.

When the patch was finished Larry came out on deck and watched the jumbled 12-foot seas that rocked *Seraffyn* unevenly about. "Let's try sailing, might steady us out," he suggested. "We can't set the main until that glue has a couple of hours to go off. But we can ease onto a reach with just the staysail."

It's surprising how that 104-square-foot sail steadied us out, not only physically but mentally as well. Now that we were sailing again, the fear of the unknown represented by that word "typhoon" was

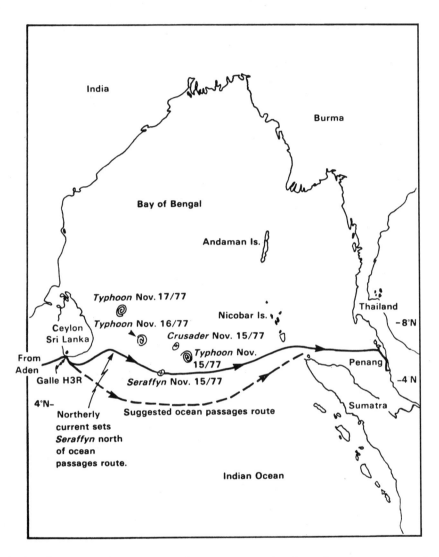

behind us. Yet that unnamed storm came back to haunt us time after time as we sailed eastward.

Two days later, as we beat tack on tack against 20 knots of wind with our two roughly patched sails holding together and setting nicely even if they did look ugly, we sat back and listened to our favorite BBC news broadcast. "Unseasonable typhoon whips across Bay of Bengal, disrupting shipping with 100 mph winds, killing at least 200,000 people in southeast India. Tides rise 10 feet above normal." It was hard to believe that was our storm. By this time the winds and seas had diminished in our minds until I concluded, "Good, strong gale." "We were on the very edge, didn't get much of a real wind," Larry agreed.

STORM MANAGEMENT

But some very sad events that occurred two months later proved us both wrong. We'd been less than 80 miles from the center of that typhoon in an area where satellite weather photographs indicated sustained winds of 80 knots.

Although our first few days near Lumut were a perfect foil to the ocean voyaging that lay both behind and ahead of us, a simple note that appeared at the yacht club brought the open ocean back into our lives with a frightful jolt. We were having a nightcap with Peter Thuell when Seaman pinned up a piece of paper. "Anyone knowing the whereabouts of the yacht *Seraffyn* please report to the port captain of Penang." All we could think of was that we'd accidentally forgotten to pay some fee, or maybe our stolen jewelry had been recovered. The next morning we both walked down to see the Lumut port captain in his side room at the post office. The Malaysian reluctantly took his feet off his cluttered desk when we came in. He dug out a copy of the note we'd seen and lazily dialed the telephone. We watched in amazement as his eyes grew wider and wider, the longer he listened to the voice on the far end of the line. He set the receiver back in its cradle, stood up, and adjusted his uniform shirt. He coughed, stuttered, then started. "Don't you know . . . I mean, you must realize . . ." Larry and I both began to lean forward in our chairs. "You are missing," the flustered man finally blurted out. "You've been missing for over six weeks!"

"What?" we chorused.

"You were reported lost in that typhoon. You went missing. Another Canadian yacht went missing. There was a search. The port captain in Penang was in charge."

"But we were anchored in front of his office for ten days," Larry said. "We registered at his office and got a deratification certificate there, too!"

The sweating man wasn't listening. "You must wait right there. Don't go beyond the square until I call for you." We could get no more information at all from the port captain, so we went out under the banyan tree, bought a slice of chilled pineapple from a vendor, and tried to figure out what was happening. "Do you suppose Don Sorte reported us missing when we didn't go to Phuket?" Larry asked.

"No, I'm sure he wouldn't have done that," I said. "We told him we might go there if we had southerly winds, but we had northerlies. Besides, didn't the port captain say another Canadian yacht is reported missing too? *Crusader* is Canadian- registered. Could be her. I can't imagine any other yachts would have been out in that typhoon." For an hour we sat and tried to unravel the threads of this bureaucratic mix-up. Then a young boy came over and told us to hurry, the telephone was waiting. Larry spoke for almost 20 minutes. When he finished he looked drained. "It was *Crusader*. They're gone, missing,all six people. That was the Canadian embassy in Kuala Lumpur. Did you know our parents were notified four weeks ago that we were lost at sea?" Larry paused and I said, "Sure glad we sent them letters from the Langkawi Islands. They couldn't have worried for too long." Larry shook his head. "Those letters didn't arrive. My parents were in touch with the embassy just two days ago. But the embassy promised to telephone direct to Canada today. I can't believe it all."

Over the next week the story gradually began to sort itself out. About once a day a youngster would find us at the club and ask us to hurry to the port captain's office for a telephone call from the embassy, the Penang port captains, and, saddest of all, from the parents of some of the young people who'd paid to sail on *Crusader* from Sri Lanka to Thailand.

It seems Sorte reported very strong head winds when *Crusader* was four days out of Sri Lanka powering toward the Nicobar Islands. Twice each day Don Sorte reported on the ham radio to contacts in both Sri Lanka and Bangkok. On the fifth day he called his contact in Bangkok and said, "Wind and sea very rough, too rough to sail, am powering towards Thailand." The next day he radio'd, "Too rough to continue. Having trouble figuring our position, taking on water, going to turn and run."

His message was far from clear, but it seemed he estimated wind speeds of seventy knots and above during those three days. For a day and a half he ran before the wind, dragging warps and old tires. On the last morning, the same morning we'd split *Seraffyn*'s mainsail in half while we lay hove-to, the Bangkok radio contact heard a jumbled report from *Crusader* giving a position and asking for standby radio contact. Her reported last position put her northeast of us by only 110 miles. From our calculations and the weather-satellite photos we later saw, *Crusader*'s last radio contact came while she was right in the center of the typhoon, while we lay hove-to on the southern side. When Sorte decided to stop powering and turned to run, he'd run right into the full force of the storm. The Bangkok radio operator contacted the Canadian embassy and when they found there were several other people from England, Australia, and the United States on board *Crusader*, they arranged an air search through the Australian Air Force at Buttersworth, in Malaysia. Pilots were in the air for 52 hours and covered over 100,000 square miles of ocean but spotted only one bit of wreckage, some pieces of yellow line and blue scrapwood. We didn't find out that the Sri Lankan officials had accidentally listed us as part of *Crusader*'s crew until we got a surprise visitor from Australia.

Bob MacDonald had called to talk to us via the port captain's office three days after this affair began in Lumut. "Can you prove my son Glen was on board *Crusader* when she left Sri Lanka?" he demanded. Larry described the young Australian, repeated the address Glen had written on our guest log, and said, "Yes, we called good-bye as they powered out the breakwater."

Three days after this conversation there was a farewell banquet for Peter Thuell at a local restaurant. It must have been after midnight when we all got ready to leave. We were standing outside on the walkway teasing Peter about the voyage that lay ahead when a tall, dark-haired man burst into our crowd. "Are you Larry and Lin Pardey?" he asked. "I've just flown from Australia. I've been on buses and in taxis all night. I hoped it was you. I didn't think there could be any other foreigners in a village this small. I must talk to you right away. I won't believe Glen is dead. I know he isn't."

Bob MacDonald had been part of the search efforts from the beginning. He stayed with us for a day and showed us the met charts he'd received, the reports from the Australian Air Force search, transcripts of radio reports. We got out our passage chart and log, then compared notes. Bob left to begin a search that included visits to Thailand, Sri Lanka, Sumatra, and Singapore—with no results. But even now, four years later, he refuses to accept the idea that his son drowned during that hurricane.

When Bob left, we called our folks just to be sure they'd stopped worrying. It was the day after Christmas. "I found you were safe Christmas Eve," my mother said. "We got a letter you'd sent from Langkawi. Why didn't you buy airmail stamps? That letter took six weeks to arrive."

That solved another part of the mystery. But to this day we wonder why two port captains in ports seldom visited by foreign yachts never connected us with the search that was supposed to cover the whole Far East. Search messages were obviously circulated, because at every port we visited after we left Lumut and until we reached Brunei, we were informed we were listed as missing.

Larry and I spent most of our evenings during the next few weeks discussing *Crusader's* disappearance. The facts we knew for sure were that *Crusader* had been taking on 50 gallons of water a day even while she lay at anchor in Sri Lanka. This was because of a leak caused two years before by a grounding on a reef near Bali. Don Sorte had tried to repair the damage with internal hull strapping going along the frames to the keel. He said he would have hauled the boat and done a more complete repair the last time he was in Singapore, but, "This new ham set cost me nearly two thousand dollars, so I was short on cash." Larry had inspected *Crusader's* lower spreaders and found rot at the inner ends. Sorte planned to repair those and the keel leak when he laid up in Singapore after his visit to Thailand. So we knew the boat was vulnerable, especially since Sorte radio'd that he was powering directly into the seas generated by winds he estimated at 70 knots. Since *Crusader* had a very heavy fin keel and flat, spoonlike forward sections, the pounding she must have been taking could have strained the defective hull-to-keel connection even more. Sorte reported having trouble getting a fix during the storm. If, as he mentioned in Sri Lanka, he rarely took sights until he was approaching his landfall, he would not have known about the unusual current that was setting into the Bay of Bengal at close to .60 miles a day. That would have accounted for his final position 110 miles north of us and 180 miles north of the rhumb-line course we'd all wanted to stick to.

There were several lessons to be learned from this tragedy. First, the crew who answered the ads for a ride to Thailand were taking a big risk by assuming that the boat was seaworthy and the skipper was competent. Only two out of the five crew on board had ever sailed before. Two others had joined the boat only two hours before it left. Had they known the boat was taking on water even in port, they might have changed their minds. Second, if Sorte had kept an accurate daily fix and followed the course set out by the *Ocean Passages for the World,* he would probably have missed the typhoon completely. Third, *Crusader's* position 48 hours before he sent the Mayday was on the dangerous semicircle of that typhoon. If Sorte had chosen to heave-to or lie-to a sea anchor instead of running, he might not have sailed into the path of the storm, where two ships reported winds in excess of 100 knots. But the most important thing we learned from all of this was never to assume the weather will be cooperative. No matter what the averages shown on the pilot charts suggest, storms can happen on any ocean at any time of the year.

The Last Leg

Each morning at 0910 we'd listen to the WWV weather advisory for the North Pacific. I'd write down the latitude of the fog bank that seemed to stretch from Alaska to Hawaii, and we'd both give a curse. Even if we altered course and dropped 200 miles south, we'd still be fogbound. Then I'd list the coordinates of any storm within a thousand miles of us. Four unseasonable depressions passed far to the north of us, marching from Russia's Kamchatka Peninsula, across the Bering Sea, and into Alaska. We could feel their progress as our winds slowly veered from south to west, then northwest, before settling back to south again. A fifth depression made a short swoop south of this track, and we'd been just inside its storm radius for a day. We'd felt sure that would be our last exceptional winds for this voyage. After all, it was midsummer.

Then, just after we moved our noon-to-noon position markers onto the Eastern North Pacific charts, a sixth depression developed that seemed to detour determinedly south and crawl along the Kuril Islands of Japan before rushing toward the tip of the Aleutian Islands. I'd been ready to turn the shortwave radio off when I heard, "All mariners stand by for further storm warnings." I waited impatiently through a minute and twenty seconds of time-tick recordings; then the announcer said, "Typhoon, speed nine knots, projected course east-southeast, radius of storm winds, 300 miles on southeast quadrant." The coordinates he read off put the center of that storm 600 miles behind and just to the north of us.

During the next hours, the wind slowly veered until it lay on our beam. The seas increased and their tops began to crumble. Spindrift streaked down the back of each towering, marching wave, and exactly one day after that first report, Larry went out on deck and rounded *Seraffyn* up to face the growing seas and shrieking wind. We lay hove-to for less than an hour before the steadily increasing wind began to sail *Seraffyn* forward out of her protective slick, even though she carried only a triple- reefed mainsail and her tiller was tied to leeward. That's when Larry decided to set the sea anchor. I put on my foul-weather gear and brought the para-anchor out with me. Then we both tied lines around our waists and cleated them to the mast to protect us as we worked on the plunging foredeck. Larry rigged a bridle while I spread the parachute-type sea anchor out on deck. Once it was rigged we fed it slowly over the rail and watched it set to work holding *Seraffyn's* bow 50 degrees from the wind. Now she lay hove-to in the slick that the 9-foot parachute and her long keel created, as the Force 10 winds shoved her to leeward. For 29 hours we lay to the para-anchor, the tiny triple-reefed mainsail steadying the boat, only occasional seas crumbling ineffectively against her hull. Every 6 hours the WWV updates moved the typhoon along a track 300 miles north of us into the Alaskan Gulf. Then, as the seas started to lose their growl, as they began to stop cresting into tunnels of green-and-white foam, the newest WWV report downgraded the typhoon to a storm, but with that good news came some bad. Two more storms were following the same track; the first would be in our area in two and a half days, the storm behind it in four.

As soon as Larry felt the seas had lain down enough so that we could safely begin reaching again, he set sail to try and get more room between us and the storms. But they moved faster than our five and a half knots, and we lay hove-to 56 hours later. This storm lasted only 15 hours, and we began to run again for 10 hours, only to get hit by the next storm, with new reports of two more depressions approaching. In all, five storm fronts blew directly over us in 11 days. We later learned that this was almost unheard of during the month of August. In fact, it caught the fishermen of Washington and Oregon completely unprepared, and 29 large trawlers with close to a hundred crew were lost as we fought our own private battles several hundred miles off the rocky shores of Canada.

My reaction to this series of storms where we'd expected good sailing was anger. I shut the radio off and refused to listen to any more weather reports. "I don't want to know where the goddamned things are. We'll feel them when they get here," I said after six days of sail, heave-to, wait, set a scrap of sail, run, then heave-to again. So I stayed in my bunk most of the time, reading, writing. In the relative calm between storms I worked like a demon, baking bread and coffee cakes, boiling potatoes and dried beans for salads, cooking up anything I could so that we'd have something interesting to eat when the next storm hit.

During those five separate depressions we had to resort to storm tactics for over a hundred hours. While I spent most of my time in the relative comfort of my bunk and got up only to heat coffee or soup, Larry seemed to get excited by the series of storms. He spent hours on deck watching the para-anchor work, tossing bits of paper towel overboard to see how *Seraffyn* was drifting. "You should see how those waves crumble when they hit our slick," he yelled down. "Come on up out of there; get some fresh air, you lazy little mole." I'd be tempted, then I'd hear another lashing of spray fly across the boat and I'd say the hell with all that wet. I think in reality I didn't want to be reminded how small our floating world really was. Below decks I felt safe; on deck the endless marching, towering waves, the scudding fog, the noise of hissing foam, and the occasional sight of the huge, silent brown albatross that had followed us for almost 2,000 miles left me feeling dwarfed and lonely.

When the second storm began to howl around us, Larry decided to try lying ahull instead of setting our triple-reefed mainsail and heaving-to. Within three hours the gale-force winds WWV reported seemed to grow to storm force. It was night, but neither of us could sleep as the boat rolled and lunged. "This is the worst we've ever been in," I said to Larry. "Can the boat take it?" He listened to the waves crashing against our bow and said, "I hope so." Then we heard a roaring freight-train-like noise. The boat lurched sideways as that wave landed on top of us and seemed to force us down into the cold, storm-tossed sea. Squirts of saltwater found minuscule crevasses around the sliding hatch and drenched the inside of the cabin. "I don't like this; I'm going on deck," Larry said as he struggled to pull on his foul-weather gear. "You be ready to hand me the para-anchor if I need it."

I could hear him working near the mast while I mopped up saltwater from the countertops and settees and tried to dry the spots where it had drenched our sleeping bags. I heard the rattle of sail slides and the crack of a flogging sail. Then, all of a sudden, the boat seemed to fall asleep. She lay at peace, heeled about 10 degrees. It was almost as if we'd sailed out of the storm into a mild gale. Larry came below about a half hour later glowing with reports of how well the boat was lying hove-to. "Lying ahull gave the boat no protection at all. She kept sailing because of the windage against her rig and hull. The minute I got her stopped, she started sliding to leeward, and her slick made those waves lose their force. You should see it. Waves are breaking forward and aft of us, but as soon as they hit our slick they crumble into foam."

Between each storm we rushed toward Canada. On our forty-fifth day at sea, *Seraffyn* was running under triple-reefed mainsail and double-reefed staysail on the edge of the ninth depression. Larry was hand steering, helping the wind vane keep us stern-on to the largest of the growling waves in 50 knots of wind. "Give me a log reading," I called out to him. I plotted our "guesstimation" and called back, "Only about 400 miles to Cape Flattery."

"If this fog doesn't break we'll heave-to at noon tomorrow," Larry called. "I'm not going any closer to the coast until I'm sure of our position." We hadn't had a sight for seven days now. Fog or low, gale-driven clouds had hidden the sun from us, and I had to agree with Larry. It would be foolish to close the coast until we were absolutely sure of our position. Currents or miscalculations could put us closer to the rocky, foggy lee shore than we thought we were. With following winds such as we had, we'd never have a chance to hear the surf before we sailed into it. We remembered one comment from the letter we'd received when a friend ran onto a reef and lost his boat near Fiji: "The worst thing was when I realized I was in the surf. I didn't have time to get the whisker pole down, then shorten sail and sheet in to beat off." If this had been an offshore wind, I know we'd both have felt less apprehensive about going closer as we waited for the fog to clear.

Section II—Questions About Storm Tactic Choices, Plus Details of Heaving-To or Lying-To

During many of the discussions we have had with sailors in ports around the world and in seminars around the United States, questions about storm management principles have come up. Some of these were about details, such as how to cut chafe on the anchor rode or how strong a storm trysail needs to be. Others have been more philosophical, such as "if professional sailors like Voss found heaving-to and lying-to so successful, why do most of the modern pundits say you can't heave-to after winds reach above gale force?" To try to answer these people concisely, we have chosen the straightforward format of this section, questions, followed by answers including relevant back-up research sources. This is a book we hope will evolve and possibly act as a forum to discuss other aspects of storm tactics for sailors. We plan to update this handbook over the next few years so that others feel more comfortable about storm preparation, for the answer does lie in preparation. Luck is involved in storm survival, but in sailing, as in life, luck seems to be biased in favor of the sailor with a plan.

Questions About Storm Tactic Choices

Q Why do you feel so strongly that running before a storm is dangerous?

A As mentioned in Section I, Miles Smeeten talks of how many people, including him and his crew on *Tzu Hang,* have had serious problems (rolled over, pitchpoled) when running, yet a careful reading of the first edition of Adlard Coles's *Heavy Weather Sailing* showed no instances of the same happening to boats lying hove-to. We have done a search of the 4th edition of *Heavy Weather Sailing,* published in 1992, including Fastnet results, and are amazed to find that in over 141 instances of boats being knocked down, rolled over, lost, dismasted, of crew being lost, only one incident happened while a boat was hove-to. (Unfortunately the account deals with the rescue problems and does not describe the method or gear used to heave-to or the attitude at which the boat was lying.) Stories in the book that give comparisons of boats that were running, lying ahull, or heaving-to should be given a special reading. During the infamous Fastnet race of 1979, in which over 300 yachts took part, the crews on 158 felt they had to use special storm tactics to protect themselves from the breaking seas. One hundred of these boats suffered full knockdowns, at least 77 reported being rolled over, some more than once. What tactics did they employ? Twenty-six hove-to under sail alone; 86 lay ahull; and 46 yachts ran before the wind and/or towed warps or other gear behind them to slow them down. None of the 26 boats listed as lying hove-to reported being rolled or suffering major damage.

On pages 141 and 142 of the 4th edition of *Heavy Weather Sailing,* in a chapter written by Adlard Coles himself (many of the chapters in editions 3 and 4 were contributed by other authors), he tells in detail of 6 of the 46 yachts that started the Santander race of 1964, in which one yacht and five lives were lost.

"Three class III yachts, *Lundy Lady, Zeelust,* and *Vae Victis,* hove-to with plenty of sea room rather than close the coast with restricted visibility, and these experienced the worst of the weather. They did not finish until Wednesday afternoon and were the last to arrive." Coles then goes on to tell about the class III yacht *Aloa,* which lay ahull for nearly 24 hours. "It was not until 1700 on Tuesday 18 August (when the weather was at its worst) that a big sea threw her on her beam ends, which stove in a part of the lee side of the coachroof and part of the cockpit coaming.

"The boat was flooded . . . her motor put out of action. At about 1800 *Aloa* shipped a second breaking sea, which once more flooded the yacht. She was pumped out again, and the skipper decided to run off to the eastward under bare poles.

QUESTIONS AND ANSWERS

"Two hours later, at about 2000, *Aloa* was struck on the port quarter by another breaking sea, and this time she was capsized. This is evidenced by the facts that the windvane and anemometer at the masthead were bent and the dinghy was caught in the cross-trees."

Three men were washed overboard, two remained attached by their lifelines and survived, but the third was lost. After attempts were made to locate him, the report continues, "the remaining crew pumped the ship dry, made emergency repairs, set the mainsail, and hove-to." Sixteen hours later the wind started to lie down, and the following evening Aloa was taken in tow by a French trawler.

Marie Gallante II, another of the class III boats, gave up the race and ran for the River Gironde about 80 miles to the leeward. As *Marie Gallante II* approached the entrance to the river, "she was struck by three heavy, breaking seas. The first smashed the transom and stove in the cabin doors and flooded her. The second capsized her and broke her mast, the third caused her to fill and sink. The owner was wearing a safety harness that was made fast to the rigging, and he went down with the yacht." In the end only two of the five crew survived.

A third yacht from this same racing class also ran for shelter instead of heaving-to. Though she did get under the lee of the land, a jib sheet parted and she was driven ashore and lost; fortunately all the crew survived.

Three yachts hove-to. One of the three running boats suffered a capsize, then hove-to. None of these boats suffered any damage while lying hove-to. This led Adlard Coles to write in his summation of this event, "It is safer to ride out a gale at sea rather than run for shelter to leeward."

Many other reports back up our feelings that sailors are losing their boats and lives by running instead of heaving-to. As you read through classic stories of disasters such as the two capsizes that disabled Miles and Beryl Smeeton's *Tzu Hang,* a common thread runs through many of them. The boat is pitchpoled while running around Cape Horn. These sailors then found themselves, in effect, hove-to and suffered no further damages. We spoke to Miles Smeeton about this during a circumnavigator's rendezvous in Southern California in 1979. He told us how his two wooden masts and their tangle of rigging ended up floating to windward of *Tzu Hang,* holding her about 50 degrees off the wind. She then lay well enough that her crew could effect major deck repairs. Miles stated the wind did not abate for quite a while after the roll over, and he did feel heaving-to would have been the best choice, "if I had realized there was a danger of capsizing."

Robin Knox-Johnston speaks of the same sequence of events, running, being knocked down and damaged, then lying in a near enough hove-to position and suffering no more damage. In his report for *Heavy Weather Sailing,* page 236, he speaks of taking three serious knockdowns while running with and without warps. The first causes *Suhaili* to lose her masts. The third occurred in a subsequent storm while *Suhaili* sailed onward under jury rig. But what is of most interest is his comment after he has come on deck to find his masts gone: ". . .Strangely enough, now that she was dead in the water, *Suhaili* seemed more comfortable, although we (a total of 4 crew were on board at the time) were being thrown about heavily, as rolling without her masts was considerably more violent. Two hours later the water was out of the bilges, the decks were cleared, and the last of the warps was streamed again, but this time from the bow like a sea anchor. We even attached the anchor to the warp and released it to its full scope of chain to add weight to try to keep us head-to the seas. The effect was only to bring the bow around about 20 degrees, but this was more comfortable than being broadside to the sea."

Another similar, crash-induced heaving-to happened in the storm that swept through the fleet of 80 cruisers and racers who were sailing from New Zealand to Tonga in June of 1994 (*Sail* Magazine, *Cruising World,* October 1994). One yacht was lost with all hands, seven boats were abandoned, three of those sank, and 21 crew were rescued. All eight of the boats that were abandoned or lost were running (in one case across the seas, but in the others with them). One of these sailors has a story to tell that goes right along with that of Miles Smeeton's *Tzu Hang, Aloa,* and *Suhaili.* We quote from a report written by Tom Linskey: "*Silver Shadow,* a well-tested 42-foot Craddock design, New Zealand Skipper, Peter O'Neill, was crewed by three experienced offshore sailors: son Murray, Richard Jackson, and John McSherry.

"We were trying to get west of the low (Peter O'Neill said in an interview), running very comfortably under autopilot with a storm jib and triple-reefed main, making 8 or 9 knots, when a rogue wave hit and capsized us 150 degrees. The starboard spreader collapsed, and the mast went. We got rid of the mast, and the boat was okay inside; she wasn't leaking; but then we did a 360. By now the waves were 15 meters plus, just enormous and breaking. We tied the wheel but the pounding broke the steering and the autopilot.

"From the bow we streamed a #4 jib tied at the head, tack, and clew on 200 feet of rope, to act as a big drogue. We put the storm trysail up on the jockey pole on the stern to help bring the boat's head around, and that probably saved us from being thrown over again."[*]

Peter O'Neill had broken his shoulder in the roll, but after letting the Air Force rescue plane personnel know of their situation, he

---

[*]In subsequent telephone conversations with Peter O'Neill, we learned that he has used heaving-to as a storm tactic for many years, both racing and cruising out of Wellington, New Zealand. he chose to run in this situation because of weather reports relayed by ham operators that assured sailors the storm would turn westward. The storm, in fact, turned the opposite way.

felt heaving-to with the drogue was keeping them steady enough so that he declined assistance for 40 hours saying, "We knew there were other boats in worse shape, and if those people weren't taken off, lives could be lost."

O'Neill did eventually decide to abandon his boat, since with no mast, a broken shoulder, no steering, and too little fuel to motor either back to New Zealand or on to Tonga once the blow let up, his responsibility was to get his crew home safely with no more delays or risks. He does comment that the rescue was probably the most scary part of the whole ordeal. "The crew of the HMNZS *Monowai,* a New Zealand Naval vessel, were superb, and put their lives on the line, but still the transfer was very, very scary; I thought we were going to be crushed against the side of the boat. My crew taped my arm and shoulder so I couldn't move, and we had our boat papers in a bag, ready to go. It was a very hard decision to leave her."

The final example of this crash-induced sequence bears repeating and sums up why we feel so strongly that heaving-to and using a sea anchor such as a parachute are definitely safer than running, reaching, or lying-ahull. In the *Drag Device Data Base* book by Victor Shane, he writes of the 39-foot, 11-inch Little Harbor class *Doubloon* owned by Joe Byars, who tried a variety of tactics in winds in excess of 60 knots off the coast of South Carolina. The seas were particularly steep, as they were blowing against the Gulf Stream. Joe Byars first ran before the wind under bare poles. It worked for a while but after taking five full smashes from astern (resulting in one crew member's being temporarily swept overboard) he changed course and put *Doubloon* on a broad reach, trying to work the boat out of the storm and the Gulf Stream. This new tactic seemed to work for a while, until three hours later when she was unexpectedly struck by a breaking wave and knocked down on her beam ends.

"Next they tried another tactic: lying ahull. With the centerboard down and windage aft, *Doubloon* lay fairly quietly some 70 degrees off the wind for four hours. Then suddenly a wave broke and rolled her completely, 360 degrees in about five seconds. Six hours later she was smash-rolled for the second time. All the crew sustained injuries and there was havoc down below.

"The next day the crew managed to improvise sea anchors, one of which consisted of a working jib with the head attached to the tack to create more drag. Two mattresses were also lashed onto the remains of the stern pulpit in order to create windage aft. With her 'sea anchors' deployed, *Doubloon* took no more knockdowns." In synoptic weather charters used to illustrate this story and from met office reports, the wind did not decrease until over 12 hours after the sea-anchor arrangement was deployed. After his experience, *Doubloon*'s owner is quoted in Adlard Coles's *Heavy Weather Sailing,* page 162, as saying he is "firmly of the opinion that [he] would rather take his chances in a gale by lying as near as possible head-to-wind . . . using a flatly sheeted mizzen and, if the bow tended to fall off, a sea-anchor arrangement of some sort."

Two other things concern us. When you are running, large waves can break on board and frequently do, to throw crew forward against the wheel, winches, or deckhouse. This leads to serious injuries, broken bones being only one. Also, if a crew goes overboard, it is almost impossible to get back to him. By the time you have turned the boat around, he may be miles astern. In direct contrast, in heaving-to the boat is stopped and no waves are breaking across it; it is unlikely crew will go overboard. If they do, it's possible to get back on board the boat as it is slowly drifting downwind.

Q Yet a lot of people have run before storms, with warps, without warps and survived some real big blows. Do you think the people you spoke of did something wrong? Should they have been towing warps? Or should they have been running faster?

A Robin Knox-Johnston in his report for *Heavy Weather Sailing,* 4th Edition, tells how, after being dismasted then spending a few days getting a jury rig set with the help of his very willing crew, they encountered yet another ". . . very serious blow and were knocked down again and the jury boom was smashed.

"This last knockdown was very worrying, as we had the full warps out at the time, and *Suhaili* has never gone over when lying to warps. Analyzing the situation afterwards, I can only presume that the sea that threw us was a rogue from the south, when the main seas were from the southwest. This was a cross-sea situation again, and does demonstrate that however seaworthy one thinks one's boat is, every small boat is vulnerable in a large sea. Later we met the crew of a French aluminum 50-foot sloop that had been a couple of hundred miles north of us, which had been (running and) similarly knocked about, but they had lost a cabin window and their deck had buckled."

Bernard Moitessier advocates running fast and steering not only to avoid the breaking wave crests, but also to avoid pitchpoling.

It is illuminating to note what the late Miles Smeeton had to say about this technique. "When Bernard Moitessier, that fine seaman, offers an opinion, it should be well considered, because he has twice sailed *Joshua* around Cape Horn . . . but his answer is not necessarily the right one for all yachts, any more than mine is, and it requires a superman to steer accurately like this through a dark night . . . Even if his theory is correct for other yachts, tired men and irregular waves are apt to defy it." (*Because the Horn Is There,* Granada Publishing, London, 1984 & 1985, Appendix, by permission.)

In every instance, advocates of running stress the need to steer correctly to avoid breaking seas, to keep the stern of the boat to the crests or at an angle to the crests. They disagree only as to the speed at which you should be running, or what you should be dragging to help you keep steering control. Unfortunately, few of us have the stamina to steer well for more than an hour or two at a time. Seasickness, fear, fatigue, the need to take a break for food or personal comfort reasons, poor visibility because of driving rain, dark or night—any can be the cause of a steering lapse that lets the boat assume a position that will end up in a broach. Tests in the big tank (the sea during a storm) and in controlled small test tanks all point out that a boat that is beam on to a sea is in far greater danger of being knocked down or capsized than when she is presenting either her stern or her bow to the same sea.

There is also the question we have posed before, the one that makes learning to heave-to or lay-to a drogue imperative for offshore sailors: What do you do if there is an inhospitable lee shore downwind? What then?

And finally, one danger that seems to happen frequently in reports of running off is loss of steering because of a broken rudder, broken steering cables or quadrants. What do you do now? All agree the safety in running lies in being able to steer well. So if your steering does fail, you must be prepared to use another storm tactic, even if it just allows you the time to fix your gear.

Q Then why do the vast majority of books written by and for today's sailors say you can't heave-to when winds are over Force 8 or 9?

A There is no simple answer to this question. But our research does seem to show a sudden transition in sailors' thinking away from classic heaving-to methods soon after the first round-the-world single-handed race (1967). Previous to this time some sailors had talked of and practiced running before storms with warps or drogues to help with steering and to slow their boats down. But it was the dramatic reports written by a few of the men immortalized by the Vendee Globe Challenge, precursor to the BOC, that caught sailors' attention. This included the best-selling book by Bernard Moitessier, which advocated running at speed and steering to avoid breaking seas.

His book coincided with the introduction of IOR (International Offshore Rule) style, light-displacement fin-keeled boats, which led to more cut-away underbodies and ever higher aspect rigs with ever shorter booms, boats that had little in common with more classic designs usually used for long-distance voyaging. These new design features meant the simple methods of heaving-to, reefing the mainsail, backing the staysail, or lying-to a trysail or reefed main alone did not work as well. As described in Section I, different sail plans, different underbodies mean different heaving-to techniques **(Diagram K).** But we surmise that many of the racing sailors, who are usually those writing

Diagram K

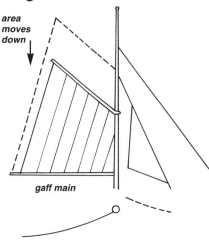

area
moves
down

gaff main

Why modern boats don't heave-to
as well as gaff-rigged vessels

Gaff cutter

Most of the area of the gaff cutter's
reefed mainsail remains aft, driving
the boat up into the wind; sometimes a backed staysail is needed
to hold the bow down a bit so that
she does not tack. Many gaffers
heave-to quite well without a staysail at all

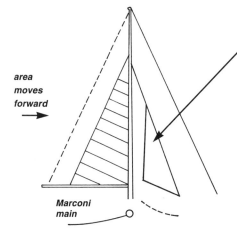

area
moves
forward

Marconi
main

Marconi cutter

Backed staysail will usually pull the
bow off, and the boat will slowly
sail beam to the wind; try heaving-
to with reefed main or trysail alone

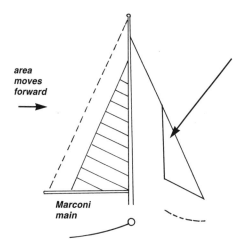

area
moves
forward

Marconi
main

Fractional sloop or
masthead sloop

The jib area moves forward a lot
when sails are reefed down. This
area forward pushes the bow off;
the sloop almost always falls off
and reaches slowly in the trough of
the waves. Try heaving-to with
reefed main or trysail alone

about storm tactics, went out and tried to heave-to in their newest to-the-rule boat and found their yacht simply tacked by itself, or fell off and began slowly sailing beam on to the seas. Conclusion: Heaving-to doesn't work on modern boats. Storms are rare occurrences in sailors' lives; races and cruises (our own included) are normally planned for the best time of the year to avoid really bad weather. So in plain words, most writers normally don't acquire the sea time necessary to experience a lot of storms. Instead they depend on other books, also written by yachtsmen, to support their storm tactics writings. In early 1995 we read the storm tactics suggestions in over 40 diffferent books, encompassing those available in bookstores and chandleries today, all written between 1975 and 1994. In each the author stated that yachts "probably" could not remain hove-to in winds above Force 8 or 9. This has led us to feel that what has happened is, when one writer with a modern boat says he couldn't heave-to in Force 8 or 9, his experience is quoted and then requoted until it becomes "accepted knowledge."

In a recent conversation with Peter Blake (January '95), we mentioned we had never heard of anyone who was properly hove-to and then felt the conditions deteriorated to the point where they had to run off. We asked if he or his friends had ever encountered such situations. His answer was a definite "No." But Peter expressed his concern that at some point the sails might begin to flog too badly or the boat, even with just the try-sail, might be over-canvassed and there would be, in effect, no other line of action. Interestingly, Peter's time to run off is hypothetical, but we do agree that without the assist of a para-anchor-type drogue to stabilize the boat, heaving-to could not be continued once the trysail was dropped.

There are other factors which may partially explain this bias away from heaving-to and toward running in storms (scudding). To racing sailors/writers, any tactic that slows them down in any way could cause them to lose the race. This would, in and of itself, make heaving-to their least favorable storm tactic. Furthermore, these writer/racers usually sail on boats with a good supply of helmsmen, so probably can run through a storm keeping the boat perfectly aligned to the following seas, steering to avoid breaking crests for hours at a time. Running through their storm would be the logical racing choice. But very few of these writers have gone out on a cruising boat with a small crew and tried the same method. The late Adlard Coles was an exception, a racing sailor who often cruised in small boats with his wife as his only companion. He speaks time and again about heaving-to in storms. In 1967 *Yachting World* magazine (UK) invited Adlard Coles to take part in a forum that included the late Eric Hiscock. We quote from *Cruising Under Sail,* by Eric Hiscock, page 375, where Eric writes ". . . Naturally the Moitessier method cropped up (running fast with no warps or drogues), and we all found it rather startling. Adlard said he had never dared to try it . . . he added that he shrank from recommending running because if it proved wrong it could lead to loss of life."

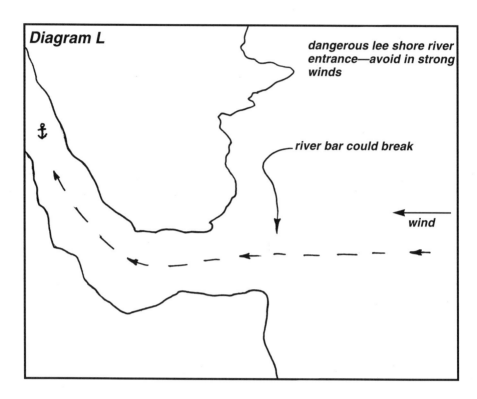

Diagram L

dangerous lee shore river entrance—avoid in strong winds

river bar could break

wind

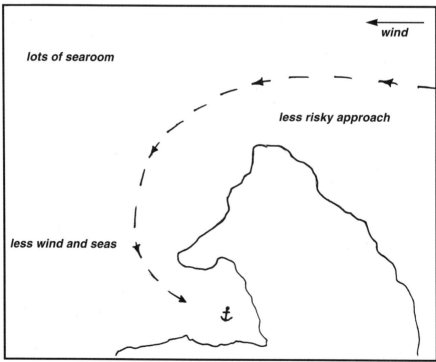

wind

lots of searoom

less risky approach

less wind and seas

QUESTIONS AND ANSWERS

Q Is there any time when running or reaching during a very strong gale would be a good idea?

A According to research conducted by the U.S. Coast Guard, British Admiralty, and from our own experiences, it appears that in the open ocean, where there are no unusual currents or shoals, even the strongest winds do not seem to cause the waves to build up to the point where they have dangerous breaking crests during the first five or six hours of a blow. This seems to be confirmed by the fact that most accounts of boats being capsized while running seem to occur several hours after the beginning of the blow. It is not wind that causes problems, but breaking seas. We have met sailors from Wellington, New Zealand, who regularly race in winds up to 60 knots. We ourselves learned to sail in winds of 70 knots and over during a visit to the Cook Straits near Wellington. But as the winds were not of long duration, the seas did not build up and gain the power to break dangerously. So if you are at the front edge of a storm that is just settling in, and if it is blowing in the direction of your goal, it is probably safe to run for three or four hours until the waves develop crests that start to tumble heavily. **The minute you even think about removing all sail to run under bare poles we firmly believe it is time to round up and heave-to.** The longer you wait, the more likely you are to encounter problems. It is better to feel you have been a bit timid than to broach and find you are in a crash-induced lying ahull situation.

Another instance in which the crew of a short-handed cruising boat might prefer to run in a developing storm is when there is shelter within 30 or 40 miles. But here you must be very careful, since giving up your sea room to run directly down to a port or river bar on a lee shore can be catastrophic, as shown by the story of *Marie Gallante II*. If, on the other hand, your final approach into harbor is as shown in **Diagram L,** one that lets you reach up to shelter, running for a while becomes a reasonable risk. We carried on rather than heave-to when we were caught in a Force 9 blow at the end of our crossing of the Bay of Biscay in late October 1974. We were only 35 miles from the lee of the protecting cliffs of Bayonna when the strongest winds hit. We were able to beam reach under storm canvas for six hours, luffing up into the seas before the breaking wave crests could hit the boat. Once we reached the shelter of the cliffs that mark the Spanish side of the Bay of Biscay, we found far lighter winds and calmer seas.

Two other times to consider running are when a storm catches you in shipping lanes, or when it catches you in the axis of a strong current such as South Africa's Agulhas Current. For here international maritime research has shown that the area experiencing the extreme waves, waves that have been measured at running up to 70 feet high with very steep faces, is along a band 30 or 40 miles wide, right near the edge of the continental shelf (100-fathom line). If by running during the first few hours of a blow you can get clear of the most dangerous part of this current and out into deep water or to shore in shallower water, running could be your best choice. But as the story of *Doubloon* (which was caught in the axis of the Gulf Stream) shows, this is not always practical.

Q What about lying ahull?

A This is the easiest possible tactic to use when a squall line hits. In fact, we usually do this when we see the snakelike line of black clouds that herald a black southeaster in the Tasman Sea or a Pompero-type wind, which is South America's equivalent. We drop all sail, secure everything on deck, then wait to see how much wind the frontal system contains, how long it looks as though it will last. But, as the seas begin to build, the notion of a boat lying ahull becomes quite uncomfortable. This is when we hoist the trysail, which brings the boat into a hove-to position and it feels as though the wind strength has dropped tremendously, as we describe in Section I. Once the waves begin to crest and break heavily, lying ahull is probably the most dangerous of the four basic storm tactics. It stands to reason that it is far harder to cause a boat to capsize when either its bow or stern is facing the sea, than when it is lying beam on to the seas. Tank tests bear this out.

From *Heavy Weather Sailing,* 4th Edition, page 352, "Stability of Yachts in Large Breaking Waves," this chapter is written by Andrew Claughton:

"It is breaking waves that cause capsize. If the yacht is caught beam-on to breaking waves of sufficient size . . . if the wave is high enough, or the encounter with it is timed appropriately, then a full 360 degree roll will be executed.

"How big do breaking waves need to be to cause this type of behaviour? Unfortunately, the answer is, not very big. During the model tests (which were carried out with the test model being aligned beam on to the waves) . . . when breaking waves were 30% of hull length high, from trough to crest, it could capsize some of the yachts, while waves to a height of 60% of the hull length would comfortably overwhelm all of the boats we tested. In real terms this means that for a 10-m. boat caught in the wrong place, when the breaking wave is 3 m. high, this presents a capsize risk, and when the breaking wave is 6 m. high, this appears to be a capsize certainty for any shape of boat. The word 'breaking' is stressed because it is these that present danger; big waves in themselves are not a problem."

He goes on to say that tests from a more sophisticated laboratory proved that the same model, lying so it did not present itself exactly beam on to the sea, could easily pass through the same crest. This

Photo 3

In trials off the Cape of Storms, near Capetown, South Africa, we were able to get this Lavarnis 36 (a close relative of the Sparkman Stephens 36) to lie comfortably hove-to in winds of 45 knots using just a heavily reefed mainsail and tiller tied to leeward. Her rate of drift was about 2 knots, as measured with the GPS of the local rescue boat. We then set the para-anchor, as described elsewhere in this handbook, and the drift dropped to .6 knots

same tank testing is discussed on page 80 of *Desirable and Undesirable Characteristics of Offshore Yachts.*

Larry, who readily admits to being anachronistic, was not keen to include the above quotes as he feels tank testing, in itself, proves little. "It is too controlled," he says. "It doesn't account for current, cross seas, windage, different boats, different crews." But after considerable debate (not always in controlled decibels) we have included this, as it is firmly backed up by our experiences and by accounts given by other sailors who have been tested in the big tank.

Photo 4

This closer look shows more detail of the pennant lead (barber haul) riding on the main para-anchor rode. We use a snatch block both here and at the stem where the anchor rode leads from the boat. There is little problem with chafe at the pennant lead attachment. But at the stem head, this can be a major problem and the line here must be inspected on a regular basis

Q Can you get most modern boats to heave-to or lie-to a large para-anchor in winds over Force 8?

A We know of many skippers and owners of modern boats who have used this tactic in storms. One of the more notable sailors is Jon Saunders of Australia, who sailed three times around the world singlehanded by way of the five southern capes in an S&S-designed 1975 vintage 34-footer. He always hove-to in storms. He did this using only a triple-reefed main with full success in various parts of the southern oceans. Another sailor, Peter Blake, the well-known New Zealander, after more than 400,000 miles of professional sailing, wrote in the introduction to the 4th edition of *Heavy Weather Sailing* telling how he hove-to in Cyclone David in the Tasman Sea in winds "going off the clock for long periods" and suffered no damage on board the modern race yacht *Condor*. That was during a delivery home from the Sidney–Hobart Race with a skeleton crew on board. He also tells of heaving-to on board his family's 34-footer in earlier Tasman storms. From conversations with very experienced skippers worldwide, including some who run charters from Cape Horn to Antarctica, from case histories we have studied, from testing we have done in South

Africa using modern boats and from comments written by Olin Stephens on this subject,* it would appear that modern boats with large skegs and rudders are likely to heave-to well using only a triple-reefed mainsail in winds over Force 8. Beyond that they may require a moderate-sized para-anchor or drogue and riding sail (trysail) aft to keep them lying steady and about 50 degrees from the wind.

More extreme underbodied boats, those with less balanced ends and/or balanced spade rudders with no skeg, will probably need the assistance of a sea anchor to hold them in the proper hove-to position at lower wind strengths than other boats.

Q Does this protective slick you've mentioned really calm seas?

A In the February 1985 issue of *Cruising World,* the professional delivery skipper Charles E. Kanter, who has had a lot of sea time on both multihulls and monohulls, wrote of his storm encounter while delivering an Irwin 37. He and his crew were caught in Force 10 winds between Great Inagua and Aucklins islands and did not have a para-anchor on board. Instead he rigged a genoa to act as a large sea anchor and lay comfortably to it. He writes, "We found that the sea anchor's being close to the surface caused the waves to break before they reached the boat, just like being behind a shoal. It was awe inspiring. Giant waves would rush up, looking like they were going to overwhelm us, and they would literally explode when they hit the sea-anchor artificial shoal. We never took green water on deck in the twelve hours we lay there. It looked a little like the famous Hawaii surf, with us standing just far enough up the beach to get a little foam."

Richard Henderson, in the 1991 edition of *Sea Sense,* writes, "In the meantime, the boat is making . . . leeway due to the fact that her keel is stalled (not supplying lift), and this causes a noticeable wake to windward, which . . . may have some effect on smoothing the seas and possibly encouraging them to break before they reach the boat. The less she forereaches and the more leeway she makes, the more effective the drift-wake to windward will be."

This same slick is mentioned in the story of *Mary T,* one of the boats that weathered the storm near New Zealand (see Section IV). She set a drogue and her crew commented that the slick was one of the most interesting things noticed.

Eric Hiscock, on page 372 of *Cruising Under Sail,* says, "The leeway creates a slick—smooth patch, such as is caused by oil—to windward, and this has some protective qualities, the crests of the advancing seas being reduced on meeting it. . . . If, however, the yacht

*"... the best available design strategy to move the CLR (center of lateral resistance) aft is to use a large skeg and rudder. These serve the functions of feathers on an arrow. Most new boats follow this pattern and if the ends are balanced they can behave well, exhibiting minimal loss of steering control, the ability to heave-to or other good sea-going characteristics." *Heavy Weather Sailing,* page 246 (1992).

Drift Speed
With or without a sea anchor

This list includes some drift rates for boats of different types, to show the contrast between lying-to a sea anchor and heaving-to with just sails. In several cases drift rates were confirmed both by classic and electronic navigation measurements.

Boat	Estimated wind speed (knots)	Drift rate hove-to, sails	Drift rate Sea anchor
Taleisin, 29' classic cutter	75–80	1.1	.6 (12' para-anchor)
Seraffyn, 24' classic cutter	gusts to 80	1.2	.6 (8' para-anchor)
Lavarnis 36, IOR type racing sloop (similar to S&S 36)	45	2.0	.6 (8' para-anchor)
Charger 33, IOR type sloop (similar to Peterson 33)	35–45	1.2	.7 (5' diameter sea anchor, cone type)
Hunter 40, modern racing sloop	winds to 45	2.0	.8 (12' para-anchor)
J/30, ultralight race boat	above 55	4.0	.6 (8' para-anchor)

makes much headway, as may happen with a fast type, or one with more windage forward than aft, the slick will be left away on the weather quarter and will then not offer proper protection."

Captain John Voss, who, before starting out on his small-boat voyages, served as master on various large sailing ships, claimed he never once shipped a sea that caused any damage once the ship was hove-to, sails trimmed, headway stopped, and the vessel making a square drift to leeward. He felt the slick was the main thing protecting his sailing ships. In his words, "the turbulent wake will then appear on the vessel's weather side, which had a most wonderful effect in smoothing down breaking seas on their approach" (from *Venturesome Voyages*).

The scientific name for the turbulent field that is formed by the succession of vortices caused by your para-anchor drogue or the keel of your hove-to boat is Von Karmon Vortex Street.* I have sat on deck during Force 10 winds and watched while almost pipelinelike waves toppled onto our slick, then crumbled into heavy foam before coming close to the boat. Yet the same pipeliners, with their overhanging crests, kept their shape and power as they broke fore and aft of where our boat lay. To write this on paper does no justice to the drama of watching the slick sap the power of the waves. Lin agrees, and the few times I could convince her to come out and watch the slick, her comment was, "It has to be seen to be believed."

Q What are the disadvantages of heaving-to or lying-to a para-anchor?

A As mentioned in the Bornholm incident in Section I, where there is heavy traffic, heaving-to seems a less attractive choice than running. But, as you have a small riding sail set aft, you can, as we had to do after broaching, heave-to and keep a good watch, then be ready to pull the tiller to windward and pay out the main or trysail sheet so the bow will fall off and the boat will resume sailing. Then you can reach, run or gybe to clear approaching traffic. Once clear, you can heave-to again. (Gybing with a storm trysail set is not traumatic and doesn't make the boat heel much when it goes stern through the wind, as the sail is controlled with sheets and not a boom.) This ability to get under way quickly is in direct contrast to lying ahull. Then, to get clear of danger you

---

*Astrid Barros N.A., who is studying the hydrodynamics of breaking waves as they affect yachts (University Federal de Rio de Janeiro and U.C. Berkeley under Professor Sergio Hamilton Spharer) confirmed that the vortices formed by the para-chute and hove-to boat can continue to disturb wave patterns for an amazingly long time, even in extreme winds. "Just take a look at the wake of a ship to see a good example of the vortex street you are trying to form by heaving-to," Astrid said when we discussed our observations with her. She was not surprised when Larry said he'd noticed waves starting to lose their power against our slick as far as 1/4 to 1/2 mile to windward from where we lay after being shoved downwind at a rate of 5/8 to 3/4 knots by 70 knot winds.

must depend either on an engine or on getting sail set, a slow process in storm force winds.

If you lie-to a riding sail and para-anchor, you cannot move out of the way of approaching ships without slipping your drogue. For this reason we set a strobe light at our masthead when we set our para-anchor. We also carry a bright orange trysail. This was suggested by Jim Marshall of North Sails, as this color is easier for ships to see than white sails, which blend in with whitecaps. (This fabric is available from Bainbridge Fabrics—ask for Storm Orange.)

Another disadvantage to heaving-to is that it is the active decision. To do it means more labor than simply taking all sail down and lying ahull or running with the wind. You must spend time preparing before you set sail, adding trysail track, getting para-anchor gear sorted out, then hanking on the trysail before you leave port, and finally at sea, raising the trysail, settling the boat down, tying off the helm, setting the para-anchor, putting chafing gear on the lines and working to get the boat to lie well. Once the boat is in position, someone in the crew must go on deck every hour to ease the para-anchor rode a few inches and spread the wear. This means leaving the cockpit and going right out on the foredeck, which, to someone who has not done so in a storm, sounds daunting. Fortunately, once the boat is lying properly, this is not a daunting task.

A final disadvantage is that, when your goal happens to lie downwind, it is very much against modern thinking to stop and wait. If you are racing, it is doubly so, since heaving-to will probably lose the race for you. But the essence of seamanship is thinking first and foremost about the safety of the ship. Art Clark, 72-year-old life-long adventurer, boat builder, and mentor, blessed *Seraffyn* at her launching by turning to us and saying, "You take good care of *Seraffyn*, and she'll take good care of you."

Details of Heaving-To and Lying-To a Sea Anchor

Q What if the head of your boat keeps falling off and she lays beam onto the seas, even with the pennant-led parachute para-anchor and a trysail set?

A There are four main things that keep boats from lying close to the wind once a para-anchor is set:

(1) There is not enough wind*
(2) There is too much windage forward
(3) The para-anchor lead is too far aft
(4) The para-anchor is too small.

In the first instance, there will normally be no dangerous seas, so it is not vital to get the boat to lie closer to the wind. But it might be more comfortable for the crew if you came into a 50 degree hove-to position, so consider the next items.

Windage forward of the mast will make your boat want to fall away from the wind. High freeboard, roller-furler headsails, staysail booms all contribute to this problem. If you can lower this windage by removing gear or furling sails from the bow area, this can help the situation. If not, you will have to set more sail area aft to counteract this windage.

You may have the para-anchor led too far aft on your pennant lead, as discussed in Section I, Diagram F. This lead should be adjustable. To get the bow to come closer to the wind, ease the pennant lead block forward.

Although the size of para-anchor will be discussed in a later question, from what we have seen, if all of the above items are covered, almost all boats will be held hove-to with moderate-sized parachute drogues. But one that is too small will not keep the head up near the wind. The old, cone-type sea anchors are an example of this. Though they cut drift a bit, they do not have enough grip on the water to help hold the bow of a boat close to the desirable position.

A final consideration in this question is special to boats with centerboards or lifting keels. It pays to experiment with the boards to see which position gives the best results. If the bow of the boat falls away, moving the board aft or maybe forward might help keep it closer to the wind.

---

*One of the difficulties of learning how to get your particular boat to heave-to with or without a para-anchor is that you need at least 30 to 35 knots of wind before you actually know how she will react to different sail combinations or pennant leads.

Q If my boat heaves-to with a trysail alone, when do I need to use a para-anchor?

A If your boat stays in the classic position and does not sail forward, away from its protective wave-sapping slick, you do not need to set a para-anchor. But we have found that at some point, most boats, including *Taleisin* and *Seraffyn* with their classic underbodies, tended to sail slowly away from the disturbed water of the slick. This usually happens when winds stayed above Force 9 and waves became high enough so that there is a variation of wind force from bottom of the trough to top. (Large sailing ships hove-to using topsails, so wave crests did not blanket their sails.) This is usually the time when sailing books advise either lying ahull or running off. To determine if you are staying within the slick, wet 5 or 6 pieces of paper towel and drop them overboard into the water on the windward side of the boat. If they appear to drift almost dead upwind from the boat, you are staying right behind your slick. If they drift at an angle aft, it means you are sailing forward out of the slick and into rough water, and it is time to set a para-anchor or drogue. Once it is set, the same wet towel test will show that you have stopped moving forward. My experience has been that once it is lying to the para-anchor the boat *always* makes a dead square drift, as shown in Section I, **Diagram E.**

   If there is reason to minimize your drift, even in winds as light as Force 4, the para-anchor is useful, even if your boat heaves-to without it. In tests we did off Gordon's Bay, 30 miles from Capetown, aided by the local rescue service and the owners of two modern racer/cruisers, a Lavarnis 36 and a Lavarnis Charger 33, GPS fixes confirmed both boats drifted over 1.2 knots to leeward while lying hove-to under triple reefed mainsails in 35 to 40 knots of wind. Drogues cut the drift dramatically on both boats. The moderate-displacement Lavarnis 36 used our 8-foot-diameter para-anchor, and drift was reduced to .62 knots. The light-displacement Peterson 32 drifted at .7 knots once a 5-foot-diameter cone-type sea-anchor was set **(Chart, page 82)**.

Q Is the para-anchor gear the same as used by many multihull sailors?

A Yes, it is, but the size of the parachute and the way the boat lies most comfortably to it is different. Multihullers usually depend on a much larger parachute with their anchor rode led from bridles attached to the bows of their hulls to hold them directly head to sea. (For more details, see *Drag Device Data Base*.) The hulls of the multihull do not therefore create much disturbance to break down seas, but the large chute does, in our opinion, create a large slick. It probably disturbs more water than a similar sized monohull would behind a 9- or 12-foot para-anchor.

QUESTIONS AND ANSWERS

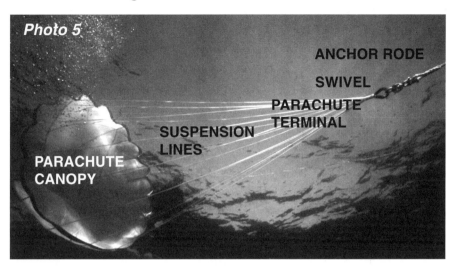

This picture is taken under water and shows a fully deployed BOURD-type para-anchor

Q What about lying directly bow to para-anchor, the way multihullers do?

A Some monohull para-anchor users report doing just that. But, as described in Section I, when we tried this, the boat rolled badly and was decidedly uncomfortable. When we tried to dampen the rolling by setting a close-hauled double-reefed main, the boat began tacking 40 degrees either side of head to the wind about every ten minutes. Each time the sail filled on the new tack, she lay nicely for a few minutes in a hove-to position. Then the anchor line pulled her head to the wind, the sail flogged, she tacked, and the process began all over again. We did not ship any heavy seas, but we did not get any rest. Without any sail set, the boat did not tack but did roll badly and felt uncomfortable in general. *Mary T*'s story in Section IV confirms this discomfort while lying head to a large drogue. Her crew reported scooping water into the cockpit on each roll. If, on the other hand, you can get the boat to be 45 to 50 degrees off on one tack without its head directly into the wind, with a small riding sail (trysail) set to dampen the rolling, the ride will be much more comfortable. Thus, the pennant-lead arrangement discussed in Section I developed.

Q What about lying stern to a para-anchor type drogue?

A Although we have not tried this method, we see the disadvantages of lying stern-to as follows:

1. The stern area of a boat, with its cockpit and companionway,

is often of weaker construction. Furthermore, green water is less likely to find its way into the boat if the bow of the boat is facing the seas. Stern to, the companionway drop boards, cockpit seat lids, and sliding hatch usually leak badly.

2. Heavy spray and the possibility of letting large amounts of water below discourage the crew from opening the hatch to come out and take a good look for ships or to check for the major worry while lying to a para-anchor: chafe on the nylon lines.

3. The fairleads and anchor-handling gear on the foredeck are usually stronger than the gear aft.

4. The para-anchor rode could foul on either the rudder or propeller.

5. If, for some reason, the parachute collapses or the rode parts, your boat is immediately in a less advantageous position, either running-off or lying beam-on to the seas. This is one of the safety features of lying-to with a trysail and para-anchor bridled off the bow. Should either the sail blow out or the para-anchor fail for some reason, you are still held nearly close-hauled, in the safest position, behind your slick. Or to put it more simply, you are using *two lines* of defense, not just one.

6. It is easier to recover the para-anchor from the bow, where your windlass is. Furthermore, you can more safely power up to relieve pressure on the rode, as there is little fear of its getting caught around your skeg or propeller when you work from the bow.

This said, if for some reason we could not lie-to a para-anchor off the bow, we would lead it through a fairlead on the stern quarter, then secure it to a jibsheet winch. The boat would then likely lie about beam on to the wind, drifting dead downwind with its slick to windward. As the story of *Mary T* shows, a storm staysail is probably needed to keep the bow of the boat off to reduce rolling, and so she lies, in effect, hove-to backwards.

Q Can you really carry sail in 70 or 80 knots of wind?

A Although fear of the unknown has kept many people from trying to set sail in extreme winds, properly built and properly sized storm sails with good leech and foot lines will definitely work in these winds. We have never heard of a Dacron storm trysail blowing out, even though we have had the privilege of meeting some of the tough men and women who race out of windy Wellington, New Zealand. They go out regularly in winds of 60 knots and over, with storm trysails as normal racing equipment—not just something to satisfy a set of regulations. We ourselves lay hove-to in 89 knots of wind off Cape Palliser (60 miles east of Wellington), using just our 9-ounce triple-stitched Dacron storm trysail, which is about 33% of our mainsail area.

It is important to remember that with a properly sized storm trysail, you have greatly reduced the area being presented to the wind. At 30 knots, the force against each square foot of sail is 3 pounds. At 60 knots it is 12 pounds. So if your boat can carry 400 square feet of sail going to windward in 30 knots without overstressing any gear (400 square feet x 3 pounds = 1200 pounds total pressure), it can carry 100 square feet of trysail in 60 knots (100 square feet x 12 pounds = 1200 pounds total pressure) without putting any more strains on your boat, though, as described in Section III, Trysails and Trysail Track, the head and tack areas of the track are subject to more strain. This is doubly true when you consider what happens as you lie hove-to correctly. If your helm is tied to leeward, the boat is pushed closer to the wind whenever a gust hits the trysail. As the boat points up into the wind, she heels less and less. This motion acts as a wind and strain reliever, just as it does when you round up in a gust under more normal sailing conditions. When the boat moves closer to the wind, the easing of pressure on the trysail lets the windage of the forward part of the hull combine with the wave action, and the boat bears away slightly again. If you get the boat lying properly hove-to, this gentle action keeps the trysail from flogging. In our experience once the sail was fully hoisted and sheeted in, it never even fluttered.

But the real question may be, not can the sails or gear take the strains, but can you actually raise the sails, be the hurdles physical or emotional. This is why a separate storm trysail track is vital for short-handed cruisers. For those who use a triple-reefed mainsail, handy pennant reefing is necessary. If the sail is easy to triple reef, or if the trysail is already attached and bagged at the mast, all you have to do is set it. For the trysail this is a simple procedure: Transfer the halyard from the head of the mainsail to the trysail, lead the sheets aft to a cockpit winch, then hoist the sail. This is a do-able task. But if you have to drag a trysail from a sail locker, then stand on the cabin top and feed it slowly into a track or mast slot on a wind-whipped deck, it becomes a formidable task.

The difficulty of setting a sail once winds reach above gale force is another reason to consider heaving-to early, instead of running before the wind. But if you wish to carry on for a while, good storm tactics would suggest that, if you are broad-reaching or running wing-and-wing with a reefed mainsail and small headsail and the wind increases, it is best to drop the headsail first and carry on with the reefed mainsail. If further reduction in sail seems in order, change down to the storm trysail. This sail will go up, even with the wind aft, as it has no headboard or battens to catch under shrouds or spreaders. On most boats under 40 feet this small sail can be winched up in storm-force winds by even small crew members. Now, with the trysail set, you are ready to heave-to. You already have the right sail up. <u>Avoid ever getting into the position that sees you running too fast under bare poles because putting up the trysail now so you can round up into the</u>

Diagram M

The most effective anti-chafe gear we have found

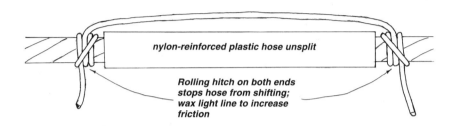

nylon-reinforced plastic hose unsplit

Rolling hitch on both ends
stops hose from shifting;
wax light line to increase
friction

Diagram N

Jury-rigged para-anchor using a jib or other spare sail

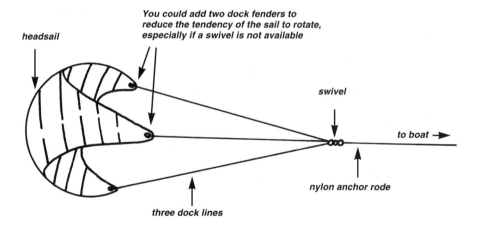

You could add two dock fenders to
reduce the tendency of the sail to rotate,
especially if a swivel is not available

headsail

swivel

to boat →

nylon anchor rode

three dock lines

<u>increased wind will probably knock her down real hard when she comes beam on to the wind and seas.</u>

Q What about the shock loads a para-anchor transmits to the boat; will the boat gear handle them?

A From our experience, which include riding out an 85-knot cyclone (Agnes) while at anchor in the Chesapeake Bay, the strains while lying to the hove-to position with a pennant to the para-anchor are not much different from what we felt at anchor in the same strength winds. We make this comparison after lying hove-to in the cyclone for 56 hours off Australia's Great Barrier Reef. If you do experience strong jerks, it could be because you do not have enough scope out, or as discussed later, you need some weight on the inboard end of the rode.

There is, however, a heavy strain on the anchor rode, and this is another reason we prefer lying hove-to facing the seas. The bow and its anchoring gear are designed to take the strains of anchor gear. You also have strong attachments here, bitts, cleats, and rollers big enough to take chafing gear to protect the rode.

Chafe is a definite problem with a sea anchor, more so than with an anchor set in a harbor, because of the extra motion caused by large waves **(Diagram M)**. If the anchor rode chafes through, you lose all your gear and the protection of the para-anchor.

Q If I do not have a para-anchor on board, and heaving-to under trysail is not working well enough, what can I use?

A As mentioned elsewhere in this question-and-answer section, a workable substitute can be made with a sail **(Diagram N)**, its three corners each secured to 30- or 40-foot-long dock lines, which are then tied to a bow line on the main anchor line to act like canopy lines and make, in effect, a triangular para-anchor; other gear can also be deployed with the object of keeping the boat in position. During the 1979 Fastnet Race the crew of the fin-keeled 45-foot *Marionette of Wight* tried to race on through the storm, but 20 miles after rounding Fastnet, her rudder broke at almost exactly the time when the barometric pressures reached their lowest readings. The crew did not like this feeling at all and worked together securing two anchor lines and three genoa sheets to form a warp almost 1000 feet long. They then led the warp over their bow, and the boat lay at an angle between 20 and 40 degrees from the wind, making what Captain Voss would call a "square drift." The crew said they then felt the boat lay steady and comfortably, though their leeway was at times as high as 4 knots. A sail drogue or a para-anchor could have cut this drift, but what is interesting is that the crew used gear on board to get this modern boat to lie safely hove-to.

91

Photo 6

Once the parachute is close to the boat, you simply hook one of the shrouds to capsize the canopy, and the water runs out. This photograph was taken when winds were gusting 35 knots, and Pat de Beer, a woman of average size by most standards, found unassisted retrieval amazingly easy

Q Should you buy a specially made para-anchor?

A Not especially. If you can locate an ordnance dropping parachute (BOURD) through a military surplus store, you can save money. The para-anchor we are using on *Taleisin*, though acquired through Para-Anchors International, is in fact a surplus chute with a 5/8-inch swivel added to it. Many commercial fishermen, who require chutes larger than those available for dropping ordnance, use surplus nylon personnel chutes. But we did note that the owner of one fleet of commercial fishing trawlers tried surplus parachutes at the suggestion of one of his crewmen. He found chutes saved him money because his crews did not feel like returning to port, as they could lie comfortably at sea during a storm and continue fishing once the winds abated. He then felt it well worthwhile investing in heavy duty, tear-resistant custom-built para-anchors.

Q What about Series drogues, Gale Riders, and other such devices?

QUESTIONS AND ANSWERS

A Each of these have proven to be successful in slowing boats down and giving them directional stability, either when running at sea or when crossing breaking river bars. But the turbulence they can create is fairly narrow compared with a hove-to hull behind a para-anchor. So they do not break the waves down as much, nor do they cut the drift as well in a lee-shore situation, unless they equal the drag co-efficient of a hull and para-anchor.

Q What size parachute anchor do I need?

A On 24-foot, 7-inch *Seraffyn* (5 tons) we used a 8-foot diameter BOURD para-anchor with full success. As *Taleisin* at 29 feet, 6 inches and 8.5 tons was about 40% larger, we opted for a 12-foot-diameter BOURD. We used it successfully in conjunction with a storm trysail in hurricane-force winds, but felt it may have been holding us more firmly than we liked, so we have since traded it for a 8-foot-diameter BOURD. It is likely that the larger-diameter parachute would hold the boat more perfectly aligned in lighter winds; some sailors have reported a para-anchor let their head fall away from the wind in gale conditions, but in these conditions a lot of boats will lie hove-to without a para-anchor. As the wind strengthens, the smaller para-anchor becomes ever more effective in controlling the boat's position.

It would be wise, however, to err toward a larger chute rather than a smaller one, and to avoid any chute smaller than 8-foot diameter for storm purposes. Tests by the U.S. Coast Guard and also by the Wolfson Unit for Marine Technology and Industrial Aerodynamics, University of South Hampton, England, show that smaller chutes may collapse more easily in rough conditions. The Wolfson report states: "Under cyclic loading, drogues and small parachutes can collapse and start to tumble so that they either cause themselves structural damage or tangle so badly as to be rendered ineffective. Larger parachutes can avoid collapse by virtue of their higher drag, causing the tow line to stretch rather than to pull the parachute through the water."[*]

A larger chute creates a larger slick and also, as mentioned, cuts drift more than a smaller one, two other good reasons to err toward the more generous size.

The only problem associated with a larger chute may be the concern of shock loading on the boat's gear. As mentioned in Section I, the open mesh of the BOURD-type para-anchor lets water sieve through under heavier loads to relieve some of the strain transmitted to the boat. We do not feel this increases the rate at which we drift downwind, as the mesh opens only momentarily under the stress of

---

[*]The Icelandic Directorate of Shipping who undertook a program of life raft and drogue testing in breaking seas found that, by fitting a net between the shroud lines and the canopy so that the space between lines and canopy are divided equally, tangling was completely eliminated.

unusual sea and boat strains. Our 5/8- to 3/4-knot drift rate, which is considered high by multihull users of para-anchors, is probably directly proportional to the size of the chute. (The recommended para-anchor size for multihulls of 35 feet is 28 feet in diameter.) The whole question of para-anchor size is still open to debate. We wonder if a larger, slower drifting chute would produce the same amount of slick, or would its larger size create even better wave-busting vortices? Only results from those who actually use para-anchors during storms will help everyone know what sized gear to choose. At the moment the following guidelines should work for owners of moderate displacement monohull sailboats:

> 20 to 29 feet—8-foot diameter
> up to 35 feet—12-foot diameter
> up to 40 feet—15-foot diameter
> up to 50 feet—18-foot diameter
> to 100 feet—24-foot diameter

Q What about rudder damage? Several writers say this is more likely when a boat is hove-to or lying-to.

A Rudder damage is more likely to occur when a boat is held directly head-to-wind with a small cone-type sea anchor. If a larger than normal wave causes the cone-type sea anchor to momentarily lose its grip, the boat can slide directly backwards, and the rudder can jam over hard enough to shear the pintles or part the rudder from its shaft. This same thing could happen if you missed a tack in heavy seas and a wave shoved the boat aft before you could get out of irons. For this reason it is a good idea to rig rudder stops, if at all possible. But once you are lying-to a larger sea anchor, there seems to be little chance of this rudder damage occurring. Never once during the times we lay directly head-to-wind using a para-anchor did we move directly astern. We had the tiller secured with heavy shock cord to act as a backup to the rudder stops, but we did feel the larger sea anchor and the slick it produced kept the boat from being shoved backwards. Even better is to lie-to a pennant lead on the para-anchor line. Almost all of the strain is then removed from the rudder as the forces from any crests that do enter the slick area tend to shove the bow of the boat sideways so it pivots away from the blow and the stern barely moves.

We do have rudder stops permanently rigged on our outboard rudder. We do use a tiller, which can be easily lashed with shock cord to dampen strains. On a boat with wheel steering, hove-to in a sustained storm, it could be wise to disconnect the steering system and insert the emergency tiller to cut down on the chance of fatiguing any part of the wheel steering system. Shock cords could then be secured more easily to the emergency tiller.

QUESTIONS AND ANSWERS

A final word on rudder damage, which seems to be one of the main arguments against heaving-to or riding-to a sea anchor of any type; we would much rather accept the risk of damaging our rudder than to lie ahull or run off and risk a knockdown, broach, 360 degree, or pitchpole, any of which could have life-threatening results.

Q What about using a tripline to make retrieving the para-anchor easier?

A Here it is definitely a case of KISS: Keep It Simple, Sailor. Some of the studies in the *Drag Device Data Base* tell of tangled chutes because of triplines. In one case the boat lay ahull because of the tangled chute and was capsized before the chute was reset. Properly or improperly rigged, a tripline adds complications to a basically simple system. So we'd rather have problems after the winds have abated, when we are bringing in the chute, than during the storm when we need the chute most. With the judicious use of an engine and a sheet winch or windlass, retrieval may be slow, but it is not too difficult without a tripline. Although some people talk of putting chain or weights near the parachute when they are launching it, we feel this is unnecessary and could make retrieval extremely difficult. The reason: As you pull the parachute in, the chain will cause it to sink. When the parachute is directly below the boat, the weight of the water in it will make it extremely difficult to winch in, in a seaway. This could also cause the bow of the boat to feel as if it is being pulled under water. Without the weights, the top edge of the parachute will float near the surface. As soon as the shroud lines are near the boat, it is relatively simple to reach out with a boat hook and catch one of the lines **(Photo 6)**. Pulling this line will capsize the chute, and the water will pour out. But in every case it pays to have a second person tail the line as you bring the para-anchor in, instead of using a self-tailing winch. This way the trailer can let the line slip if a passing wave puts a heavy strain on it.

Q What about adding weights to the para-anchor line to cut down jerking motions?

A If the para-anchor is let out so that both it and the boat are approximately at the same part of successive waves as the same time, we have never experienced any excessive jerking. Other users have mentioned this and said it eased when they let out more line, up to 400 feet in some cases. But not all of us carry this much line, and logic would suggest that by adding weight to the anchor rode, a catenary affect, just like that of chain with a normal anchor, can be achieved to cut down jerking. Larry has considered ways to do this should we encounter worse conditions than those we have seen so far. He plans to remove the chain from the bow anchor, then secure the anchor chain to the inboard end of the para-anchor rode with an antichafe device (thimble or heavy-duty plastic hose), then ease out sufficient chain so the para-anchor and boat are almost at the proper position in regard to successive waves. Then he would tie a line, using a rolling hitch, onto the chain, and fairlead this back to a sheet winch. Then it would all be handled just as shown in Section I, Diagram F. A disadvantage to having the chain inboard is that if you wish to add more scope, you have to cast off the pennant line and secure a new one once the scope is let out. On the other hand, this chain addition eliminates the possibility of chafe on the nylon rode.

Q What else can you do to cut down on chafe?

A The best antichafe gear we have found is criss-crossed, nylon-reinforced thick wall plastic hose. Each of our mooring lines and our nylon anchor rode already have two pieces of this hose on them, ready to be moved along and secured in place (see **Diagram M** for securing method). Since our personal worst encounter off the coast of Australia, we have acquired an oversized 4½-inch sheave diameter snatch block to use as a fairlead block. This should help to reduce chafe on the anchor rode at the bow. Also, as mentioned elsewhere, the lines should all be monitored regularly and eased a foot or so to spread wear or chafe.

Q Have you had any other problems while lying-to a para-anchor?

A The only problem we have had that was not discussed in Section I occurred during the storm on the continental shelf, 50 miles east of Australia's Great Barrier Reef. At one point during that time, as we lay-to the 96-foot trysail and pennant lead 12-foot-diameter para-anchor on board 29-foot *Taleisin,* a combination of circumstances caused the bow of the boat to tack through the eye of the wind. This did not endanger the boat, but here is what Lin told me about her experiences, when I came below decks after sorting out the problem: "I was asleep in the leeward pilot berth with no lee cloth set (yes I know, Larry, you did ask me to put it up, but it makes me feel claustrophobic). That unexpected tack threw me across the cabin and I really bruised my ribs and chin. My teeth put a dent into the woodwork of the ice chest, and, to make matters worse, before I could move, the coffee pot leaped free of its restraining bars and emptied the grounds into my hair. To add insult to injury, the pot also put an even bigger dent into the varnished teak face of the ice chest, only two inches from my tooth dent."

Another result of the unexpected tack was that it put the anchor rode under the bobstay (*Taleisin* has a bowsprit). Though we were in no immediate danger, I felt I had to get back on starboard tack before the bobstay could chafe into the line. To tack the boat, I first dropped the storm trysail, then let go the pennant line, and soon the boat headed directly into the wind and proceeded to tack back onto starboard. (We have found that the para-anchor led directly off the bow causes the boat to tack from port to starboard and back, about every ten minutes in storm force winds.) To reset the pennant lead, I got Lin to stand by the pennant line on the sheet winch. I then eased about 30 feet of para-rode quickly; Lin winched in the slack to pull the para-rode aft, as shown in Section I, Diagram F. I then rehoisted the storm trysail using the halyard winch. I adjusted the helm more toward the centerline of the boat, then pulled the pennant line aft until the boat lay another 10 or 15 degrees off the wind. During the remaining 20 hours of the cyclone, she never tried to tack again.

What caused this tack? The waves, which were blowing against a two-to-three knot Australian current, were exceptionally steep, and as the boat crested each one, the wind pressure on the trysail was briefly stronger. My theory is that a large, steep wave swept past and pushed the boat's stern to leeward just as she rose over the crest of a wave. There, stronger wind, hitting the trysail, served to drive her up into the wind just long enough for her to tack. Since this happened only one time, I cannot give any firm conclusion. But I did feel good about getting her quickly back onto the correct tack. I also have now acquired a smaller para-anchor (8-foot diameter) which I plan to try out; it is possible it would not have held as firmly as the 12-footer did, and therefore might not have pulled the boat's head through the wind.

Q Is heaving-to really comfortable, and what about riding-to a para-anchor?

A Comfort is, of course, a relative thing. It comes partially from being able to keep dry, being able to get something hot to eat, being able to rest, but most of all from feeling the boat is as secure as possible. The comfort difference between lying ahull and heaving-to has been described in Section I. Adding a para-anchor in storm winds does not seem to increase physical comfort over riding just to a storm trysail, but this may be because winds and seas have increased further, so things are rougher. I can state that with a para-anchor set in cyclone force winds, we each were able to sleep for up to two hours at a time, to each get 8 hours of full rest; we also got some food heated. Peter O'Neill, whose story appears earlier in this section, received a broken shoulder during the roll-over that convinced him to set a drogue and lie hove-to. According to his story, he could feel the broken bone grinding each time he moved. But once he got the boat lying the way he wanted it, he felt the motion was good enough that he was willing to delay for 40 hours before opting to leave his ship as he felt other yachts were in greater danger than his.

Our best answer to this question is to get out and try heaving-to in Force 7 or 8. This will show you the increase in the level of comfort.

Q What other uses does heaving-to or lying-to a para-anchor have?

A Several of these have been mentioned in Section I. But a major use was indicated by the Fastnet Race rescue efforts. It is very difficult to lift an injured person off the deck of a boat with the mast swinging about. Helicopter crews cannot lower gear without fear of its fouling in the rigging. Add a para-anchor on a pennant lead and the boat should steady out. This could also help if rescue is being attempted by rubber boats coming alongside. By slowing drift and cutting roll, rescuers can more easily transfer injured crew to rescue craft.

Heaving-to with or without a drogue can also improve the quality of your cruising life if you sail through frontal system areas. As mentioned before, by heaving-to you can often let a front pass over you. But by running at, say, 6 knots when a front is moving at about 6 knots, you theoretically could stay with the front for several days or until it dissipated, and therefore you would suffer as long as possible. Since our home base is in New Zealand and we almost commute to Australia across the Tasman Sea, we have to face up to the fact that on most crossings we will have at least two or three southwesterly fronts to contend with. By heaving-to just as each front arrives, we have come to find these passages less traumatic. When we are traveling westward, the fronts arrive as headwinds, then shift to the south as they pass, slowly freeing us so we can reach onward. By heaving-to and waiting an average of 10 to 14 hours, we avoid the beating and sail reductions that are, at this stage of our sailing career, getting a little boring. We spend a relatively comfortable night catching up on our sleep, then have a fair wind the next morning (these fronts always seem to catch us just at dusk). Going eastward, we still heave-to if a strong front catches us. If the winds are less than 35 knots we usually run back off onto our course; if they are stronger we stop and let the front pass over us before carrying on. Yes, it does mean we take a day or two extra to make these crossings, but we are not racing, so we see little problem here.

Jill Knight, an Australian singlehander who has been cruising for seven years on the classic New Zealand cutter *Cooee,* learned about heaving-to only two years ago, as she was preparing to cross the boisterous Indian Ocean. "Why didn't anyone tell me how to park my boat before? I just got tired of moving so fast; I wanted a day off. I hove-to and it was just great."

Finally, this whole system can be very useful if you have gear problems. As it helps steady the boat, you will probably have more patience to do a better repair job.

QUESTIONS AND ANSWERS

We hope these questions and answers cover any doubts you have regarding heaving-to. Now we have a question to ask. Why do we rarely hear from the more successful people in our sport of cruising, sailors who have ridden out major storms with no damage, little drama. These people could tell us a lot about systems that actually worked. Why instead are the majority of articles and reports devoted to the trials of those who suffered heavy damage or loss of life?

We know these stories are more dramatic and easier to define; the people who suffered are easier to interview because they have returned to the nearest port, while those without damage sailed off to work or to finish their cruise. Furthermore, it is obvious that any sailor caught out in the same storm and suffering little damage using some other tactic would be reluctant to say how well he did. Instead he/she would say something like "I was lucky" or "I probably wasn't in the very center of the blow as they were." But I wonder if the sailing community is learning as much as it could about storm management from reticence such as this. A case in point is the magnificent story of Alain Catherineau who sailed his French-built 36-foot Sparkman & Stephens–designed yacht *Lorelei* in the infamous '79 Fastnet. He lay with only his triple-reefed mainsail set when the winds and seas reached their worst. His crew spotted flares, then a life raft with five men in it. On page 201 of *Heavy Weather Sailing* is the story of his reaction: ". . . at first he tried to get to the life raft under triple-reefed mainsail, but he was traveling too fast. . . . He started his 12-hp engine and lowered his mainsail. He then found he could not make into the seas under power and had great difficulty in turning through the wind to effect the rescue, but he could make across the seas to the disintegrating and unstable raft. The engine, with its variable pitch propeller, gave him the vital control needed to attach a line." With the five additional rescued men on board, *Lorelei* lay with her bow toward the wind until the wind abated, then her skipper took her on to the finish line. When Catherineau was asked about his success in weathering the storm and rescuing the crew from the life raft, the only comment recorded in any report we have been able to find is that his boat was of a good heavy-weather design. Our question is, Why didn't reviewers and yachting writers press him for information on what tactics he used to keep his boat safe, and if they did ask, why wasn't this published? Although details of the actual rescue are of interest, details of his storm tactics before and after the incident could help prevent the need for rescues such as he performed (good on ya, mate!).

Section III
Checklists for Storm Management

The following checklists should help you think through decisions as you select a boat for cruising, then outfit it. Checklists also outline the procedures to consider as a storm approaches and when the winds actually increase. These lists are not inclusive guidelines; many of the general items, such as carry a medical kit and set up good lifelines, are already so well covered in books by people such as Eric Hiscock and Don Street that we felt they did not need to be repeated here. What we have tried to include are items often overlooked by cruisers, plus special guidelines that make heaving-to work well.

Some of the design considerations, such as small cockpits and extra strong companionway boards (shutters) become less important if you learn to get your boat hove-to behind its protective slick, since in this position it is far less likely that serious green water will come on board. But there may come a time when you need to beat off a lee shore or, as we felt we were forced to do in the Baltic, run for clear water. In each of these cases, the chances of a knockdown are possible, and you must prepare for this eventuality. Even if you plan to sail exclusively in tropical tradewind areas where storms are less frequent, these precautions could help you feel the squall you rode out lying hove-to near Bora Bora was exhilarating and confidence building because everything worked just as you'd planned. But let one item break, let one locker full of gear fly across the cabin and cause an injury, and that same squall can become a morale reducing storm, one that makes the idea of voyaging farther less appealing.

Checklist 1
Choosing the Boat

If you have not yet acquired the boat you will use for cruising, here are some design and construction details you should consider to increase your feeling of security in storm force winds at sea.

1. Size—In 1992, Olin J. Stephens II wrote, "If structure and handling are sound, the larger design demands more from the builder and crew as the loads increase geometrically with size. Big sails supported by great stability require strength and skill to control; small sails can be manhandled. Similar observations apply to hull, spars, and rigging."

This famous designer's comments are, from our experience in delivering bigger boats, very true. Another reason the smaller boat may be the more successful choice in storm conditions is that it is easier to inspect, maintain, and renew all of the necessary gear on a smaller boat, simply because there is less of it and it costs less to replace.

2. Keel connection—Avoid narrow fin configuration underbodies. The connection area between the ballast keel and hull is too limited to provide long-term guarantees of water tightness. From reports of the major mishaps during around-the-world races, most people have heard of the keels that fell off maxi-racers at sea. What few people hear of are the repairs necessary between each leg of the Whitbread Round-the-World Race and the BOC, where crews work to stop leaking caused by keel movement along the bases of these short, narrow fins. The possibility of leaking or of keel loss would definitely make you feel less secure about facing storms at sea.

3. The rudder, to be durable and strong, must have three connection points. A skeg- or keel-hung rudder usually does have three gudgeons and pintles (bearing points). A spade rudder usually has only two. This makes it far more vulnerable to breakage and jamming, just where the shaft enters the hull.

4. Look for a small cockpit and large drains. Traditionally, the guidelines here are the cockpit, when full to the top of the coamings, should be carrying no more extra weight than the weight of a normal compliment of the cockpit crew members.

5. Ideally, the lower edge of the companionway should be higher than the top of the cockpit. This way water in the cockpit cannot be funneled below decks if the companionway boards break or are not in place.

If the companionway is lower than the cockpit edges, you must fit separate, lock-in boards that are strongly backed so they can stay in place even as a crew enters or leaves the companionway during a storm.

6. All hatches should be on centerline so they are less likely to take on water in a knockdown.

7. There should be easy access from cockpit to side deck, so crew can go forward quickly to handle gear on the foredeck.

8. Avoid large windows. They usually weaken the deckhouse structure, even if they are protected by storm boards.

9. Avoid plastic opening portlights; we have had several reports of these breaking during a knockdown.

10. Look for a low deckhouse to cut windage. Furthermore, lower cabinsides are stronger and less likely to fracture in a knockdown.

11. Choose a removable or fold-down dodger to cut windage. If the dodger is to be left in place, it should have "break-away" lashings securing it so that when it is hit by heavy water the fabric will let go to relieve the pressure. We have heard of waves smashing against dodgers and bending the whole frame so that it jams the sliding hatch shut.

12. Choose either tiller steering or a boat arranged so there is immediate access to on-deck, backup tiller steering. One of the most common failures during rough weather is metal fatigue in the steering cables leading to the wheel.

13. Look for clear side decks with at least 12-inch-wide walkways. Try crawling along the length of the side deck of boats you are considering. If you have to struggle around inboard shrouds, this may prove a problem in a real blow.

14. Look for strong rigging. The rule of thumb for safe, long-term, long-distance voyaging in the tropics is that any two shrouds (safe working load) should be able to lift the total weight of the loaded boat. This allows margin for the normal wear and tear of cruising.

15. Avoid fractional rigs that are dependent on running backstays. Running backstays for intermediate staysail stays are fine, though, and could be helpful if the permanent backstay fails for some reason.

16. Look for amidships storage space for any hard dinghies or inflatables. Don't plan to store them on the foredeck or on stern davits. Large

seas can easily wipe them off the bow or stern. Furthermore, a dinghy stored on the foredeck can get in the way of handling storm sails and para-anchors.

17. Look for cockpit storage space for any life rafts. The two most commonly reported losses from knockdowns or capsizes are life rafts stored on cabin tops or foredecks and dodgers ripped to shreds or bent completely out of shape. You could avoid these problems by heaving-to a little sooner, but in the hypothetical, ultimate storm, it is better to have them out of the way.

Checklist 2
Preparing the Boat

This list does not include obvious items such as good handholds throughout the boat and on deck, nor thermos jugs to keep hot soup ready for a storm-tossed crew. These are well covered in other books. Instead we have included items that seem to have been either overlooked or too lightly emphasized. These are items that seem to give problems not only on boats included in this workbook, but also on those we have seen during our years of voyaging.

1. Add flotation foam to the mast if it is not a wooden spar. Reason? Any alloy or glass spar can fill with water in a knockdown and could promote or prolong a complete roll over. If you are dismasted, there is a better chance you could recover your mast with positive buoyancy.

2. If you have a dodger or store your dinghy on deck, use screws that will pull loose to mount them. Do not use bolts and washers through the cabin top. It is better to lose the dinghy or dodger than to end up with a large hole in the cabin top when a wave rips them loose.

3. Find belowdeck storage spots for every piece of gear you keep on deck during normal weather. Otherwise consider any gear that is stored on deck as throw-away items, and be mentally prepared to get rid of them if necessary (see Section 1, Storms and Cruising, for more on this item).

4. Have a large manual bilgepump (2-inch diameter Edson) that can be operated from belowdecks to back up any electrical or engine-driven pumps. Be sure you can clear the strum box or add a swing valve at a T so you can switch to another intake if the inaccessible strum box clogs. Consider a longish, wandering intake hose if your boat has separate sump areas.

5. Add a second track for a storm trysail on any boat over 28 feet, and build a sailbag that allows the trysail to be stored in a ready-to-use position on the cabin top. For boats under 28 feet, an extra strong triple-reefed mainsail will be okay, but be careful to strengthen the track connection with extra fastenings where the head of the reefed sail rides.

6. If you use a roller-furling headsail, install a second stay behind the headstay for a storm jib that can be set on hanks with its own halyard.

7. Install two heavy-duty lugs or eyebolts port and starboard on or near your bow roller. These lugs should be designed to take the side loads

of the bow fairlead snatch block.

8. Install locks or holddowns on all deck boxes and cockpit lockers. Make sure the drains from these lockers do not lead inside the hull.

9. Install lockdowns on all floorboards and lockers in the crew area.

10. Add positive restraints so your gimbaled stove cannot get loose even in a roll over.

11. Check the installation of your water tanks, especially if they are amidships. They must be bolted directly to the hull or bulkheads and not just screwed in place to the fronts of the cabinets or bunks. (One cruising family chose to abandon their boat in the Coral Sea two years ago when a knockdown caused their water tank to break through the settee cabinetry. This was on a classic, well-recommended cruising boat, built by a reputable U.S. manufacturer. The tank flew across the cabin and smashed the table, far bunk, and owner's wrist on the way. We have checked out several other boats and seen this same potential problem).

12. Consider sealed gel-cell batteries and check your batteries' hold downs.

13. Try to make your boat unstoppable, even if water gets into your electrical system and shuts it down. Have a backup shortwave radio receiver, backup lighting system, dry cell or oil lamps, backup navigation such as sextant and the 249 tables. If you are in a serious knockdown, count on your electrical system's failing.

14. If you have a solar panel, have a separate gel-cell-type battery and ways to isolate these from the main system so that you can keep a light going inside the cabin if the main system packs in.

15. Have a para-anchor on board with a swivel, or have a plan for jury-rigging a sail drogue, as discussed earlier.

16. Have at least one chafe-free 300-foot nylon anchor rode of at least 1/2-inch diameter. Carry larger diameter line if at all possible. The larger the diameter, the less chance there is of chafing through the line. (We carry 5/8" diameter on *Taleisin*, and had the same on *Seraffyn*.)

17. Have a backup sea-anchor rode of at least 250 feet.

18. Carry extra snatch blocks, plastic hose for chafing gear, several shackles, and, if the para-anchor does not already have one, a large swivel.

CHECKLISTS FOR STORM MANAGEMENT

19. Carry spare foul-weather gear, as dry people keep warmer and are more able to function and think well in difficult situations.

20. Make sure every locker inside the boat has drain holes to the bilge.

21. Consider ways to be sure all oil is removed from the engine tray. The most difficult clean up of all after any major intake of water from a knockdown, or even just a good dollop of water coming in, is from sump oil spreading into other parts of the boat.

22. Buy a supply of children's modeling clay (Play Dough, plasticine) and keep it handy for stopping up small leaks that always seem to develop during a storm. It sticks to wet surfaces yet comes away clean when the blow is over. You can use this clay to make a gasket inside your chain pipe cap also, a common source of leakage during a blow.

23. Make a checklist of storm preparations specific to your boat and have a copy available for crew to use as a storm approaches.

Checklist 3
Preparing Yourself

P eter Pye, who made some wonderfully adventuresome voyages with his wife in a 28-foot cutter back in the 1950s, had a favorite saying: "In order to be a sailor, you have to go to sea." This still holds true—the more you get out sailing before you go cruising, the better. You'll know your boat, your gear, and yourself as a sailor. Here are some other tips to help you gain confidence as storms enter your life.

1. Join local racing series and cruising rallies. This way you will be encouraged to sail in strong winds. You will also learn to think of your boat as a sailing machine first. Start lines and turning marks will also help you learn to sail under a bit of pressure.

2. Charter in the Caribbean or Aegean so you get experience sailing in heavier winds. When you learn that many people enjoy sailing where winds blow 30 knots or more every day, your concept of heavy winds will change. If you ever have a chance to visit South Africa, take a week to join one of the Durban-based sailing schools, where classes are not canceled even during the almost weekly frontal systems that blow at 45 knots or more. To help you feel better about the real odds you face when heavy winds approach, here is an interesting fact. The Ocean Sailing Academy of Durban has had over 15,000 students learn to sail right around the Cape of Storms in the Agulhas current, week in, week out, winter and summer, without one major accident. Only forecasts of winds over 50 knots will cause classes to be confined to sailing inside the harbor.

3. Next time you are out sailing in winds over 15 knots, think of chores to do right at the bow of the boat while you are going to windward. Do this in progressively stronger winds, rougher seas. This will help you practice working and moving around on a moving boat. (All of us have a tendency to prefer staying in the comfort of the cockpit in these conditions.)

4. Practice removing your roller-furling sail from its groove in a fresh wind. Develop a plan to secure it, should the furling line break or the bearings in the drum jam.

5. Research and read reports of the extremely high percentage of cruising sailors who did come safely through major storms. Even in the infamous Fastnet race of 1979, over 3000 people survived, and the 19 who died did so after abandoning their boats. Most of these boats were later

recovered. In the New Zealand storm of June 1994, only 7 of 80 boats reporting from the same area were abandoned; three of these boats were left for reasons other than fear of sinking (only one of these boats sank because of the storm). For miles actually covered, as we look back over our years of voyaging and compare the number of friends injured or lost offshore to those involved in serious or fatal road accidents, we (and many other experienced sailors) feel sailing is still *much* safer than commuting on the freeway.

6. Learn as much as you can, but remember that the chances of meeting a storm during an average voyage is about 3 percent if you plan your routes and seasons carefully.

7. Finally, most people worry about how they will actually cope in a storm situation. The following quote from Robert Louis Stevenson is worth remembering:

"It is commonplace that we cannot answer for ourselves until we have been tried. But it is not so common a reflection, and surely more consoling, that we usually find ourselves a great deal braver and better than we thought. I believe this is everyone's experience . . . I wish sincerely, for it would have saved me much trouble, there had been someone to put me in good heart about life when I was younger; to tell me how dangers are most portentious on a distant sight, and how the good in a man's spirit will not suffer itself to be overlaid and rarely or never deserts him in the hour of need."

Checklist 4
Tactics as the Storm Approaches

1. If you are anywhere near land and there is any doubt you can reach a safe port before the blow sets in, *alter course immediately* to head offshore and gain searoom.

2. If you are near the equator and hear reports of a tropical cyclone in your area, head toward the equator. Cyclones rarely come within 4 degrees either side of the equator; very few have been known to cross it.

3. Get a text that discusses tropical and extratropical cyclone avoidance tactics and how to determine if you are in the safe or dangerous semi-circle. Then consider the safest direction in which to head during a storm's approach to avoid the center. The discussion on tropical and extratropical cyclonic storm tactics from Bowditch, *American Practical Navigator,* is included at the end of this handbook as an appendix.

4. If you have less than 24 hours' warning of a storm's approach, prepare to heave-to when the winds increase to 35 knots. Evading action at this time may do little good as predictions of a storm's actual path may be incorrect.

Checklist 5
General Storm Preparation

1. Check all gear on deck that may be required during the storm; clear any additional gear off the deck and secure it below. Set up the trysail, inner stay for storm staysail, any extra lifelines you feel will help. Do this early; if the storm does not materialize, it is easy to replace items later.

2. Cook wholesome food such as fresh bread, soup, stew. Set out enough easy-to-eat food to sustain the full crew for 48 hours so no one has to rummage through lockers to find it. (On *Taleisin* we have an easy access locker that is kept stocked up for rough-conditions eating—dried fruits, nuts, containers for storm provisions.)

3. Make up a pack of dry clothes and towels for each crew, and seal them well in two layers of plastic, just in case large amounts of water do get inside the boat.

4. Clean up inside the boat. During the height of a blow, the inside of the boat will tend to get cluttered with foul-weather gear and wet clothes, so start out organized to keep crew morale up.

5. Put all locker and floorboard securing locks in place.

6. Either remove roller-furling sails from headstays, or—a definite second choice—twist a spinnaker halyard around them like a maypole, to keep the sail from coming loose during the blow.

7. Check bilgepumps and their intakes.

8. Check alternate lighting systems and flashlights. Put spare batteries in an easy-access locker. Have a separate strobe light with a system to hoist it should your masthead strobe fail. Check its batteries (see *Self-Sufficient Sailor,* page 117).

9. Minimize radio discussion of oncoming storms, as this often raises your crew's apprehensions. The time you spend on the radio could probably be used to more advantage preparing the boat and your crew for the blow and by getting more rest before it arrives.

10. Have the crew mark an hourly DR position update on the chart. If your electronic navigation methods get wet, you at least have a clue as to your location. Note any dangers within 100 miles of your position and the direction in which they lay, so if it is necessary to heave-to you

can choose the tack that will help you increase your sea room.

11. Write the barometric pressure reading down hourly. The speed at which it drops will indicate the intensity of the blow in most cases. In the unusual situation in which a low pressing against a ridge of high pressure gives little warning of a developing blow, monitoring the barometer will let you know when the situation is likely to improve.

12. Start watches immediately to get each of the crew as much extra sleep as possible, even if it is not yet night.

Checklist 6
When It's Time to Heave-to

Once you have rounded up into the wind, as discussed in Section I, Heaving-To, and have dropped all sail other than those you will be using to keep the boat in position, here are the steps we follow:

1. If using a triple-reefed mainsail, check and tighten the topping-lift to support the boom and help reduce the strain on the sail's leech. Do not lift the boom too much or the leech of the sail can flog. Check the leech of the sail for flutter, and tighten the leechline to stop any movement. It is better to keep the line too tight than to risk fatiguing the sail cloth.

2. If riding to a trysail, lead the weather sheet over the boom and forward of the lazyjacks so the sail can be sheeted in on the other tack if and when required (if the trysail is secured to the boom instead of to its own sheets, proceed as in item 1).

3. Double check to see that sheet leads are clear and will not chafe.

4. If lying-to a triple-reefed mainsail, now is the time to check the clew outhaul pennant for chafe. Add an additional tie-down through the reefing clew and around the boom as breakage insurance. If the clew lets go, the main will tear along the tied-in reef-points just like a sheet of paper toweling.

5. Check your mainsheet and traveler control lines to make sure they are secured with extra turns onto the cleats so they cannot come loose. If they do come loose they will let the boat lie ahull. If you normally use jam cleats for either the mainsheet or the traveler, relead the lines to regular cleats. The jam cleats can chafe into the lines in these conditions.

6. If you are using a trysail, now is the time to add extra gaskets to secure the furled mainsail in place. Shockcord gaskets are not secure enough; instead use at least one nylon webbing gasket every two feet to insure the sail does not get loose.

7. Tie the storm jib or storm staysail securely to the anchor windlass, or remove it and stow it below if you do not have a windlass to use as a tie down. Sail bags lashed along the foredeck are at risk; they add windage where you don't want it and can get washed away during the blow.

113

8. If you are riding to the trysail or triple-reefed main, and the barometer begins to fall, now is the time to prepare the para-anchor gear, before the increase in wind arrives.

9. Fold down dodgers to reduce the windage. Lock the drum on any roller-furling gear with a shackle or pin. This lock must be positive, as the vibrations in strong winds cause chafe on furling lines at the fairleads. If at all possible, get the sail off the headstay. A roller-furling sail loose in a storm can lead to serious consequences.

10. Any spray dodgers that are not seized in place with light cotton line along the top and vertical lashings should be removed now. The light line acts as a breakaway point should a wave hit. If you have used synthetic line, the force of a breaking sea against the cloth could flatten your lifeline stanchions and tear holes in the deck of your boat.

11. Tiller-restraining shockcords should be doubled up. Tie four $3/8$"- or $7/16$"-diameter shock cords to the tiller, or to the wheel, two for each side. Secure them with a round turn, then a bowline, which tightens securely (other knots slip or loosen). The outboard ends should be turned three times around a sheet winch and cleated firmly. We repeat *firmly* because shockcord likes to untie itself as it works and stretches. Your second set of shockcords should be a bit looser than the first, so if the first breaks or unties, the second set takes over.

12. Tie off the halyards to stop all noise possible. Noise not only represents wear and tear, but also keeps sailors awake.

13. Secure your windvane as necessary. We remove our windvane cover and put restraining lines on the trimtab to reduce wear. With Aries-type vanes it would be wise to remove the plywood vane and possibly the rudder blade.

14. Observe and record your average compass heading plus wind direction. A wind shift can let you know where the center of a cyclone lies (see appendix).

15. If the wind and waves increase, the boat may begin ranging about; i.e., it will tend to head up closer to the wind, then fall away, or it may just sail forward away from its slick. If this happens, it is time to set the para-anchor, which will stabilize the boat and stop its headway. (We feel it is far better to turn the boat into the wind by heaving-to than to try to deploy a para-anchor while running.)

16. To set the para-anchor, take the para-anchor forward and handle it as you would your spinnaker. In other words, tie the bag to the weath-

er shroud if it is a heavy-fabric chute, such as the BOURD. (This type of chute can be launched easily by sliding it down the topsides to windward. If you are using a lighter fabric chute, wet the fabric down first; then slide it over the windward side to launch it.)

17. Remove the nylon anchor rode from the hawsepipe and lead it through its snatch block on the bow, then outside of the pulpit and clear of lifelines and shrouds to shackle it to the chute's swivel, which should be available in the mouth of the chute bag. Be absolutely sure the lead is correct; a foul up could cause the anchor rode to chafe quickly. There will be as much pressure on the line while you are setting it as there is on a steel anchor being set into a hard mud bottom in an onshore anchoring situation.

18. Next, arrange the pennant line on the windward side of the boat so its snatch block encompasses the bow anchor rode. Adjust the length of the pennant line so the pennant block is about halfway between the mast and the stem of the boat. Lead the pennant line aft through a hawsehole or strong fairlead and add chafing preventors wherever necessary so it leads onto your windward sheet winch.

19. Pull about 50 feet of slack into the main anchor rode through the pennant block, then secure the rode at the bow. Take the chute out of its bag and slide it overside, canopy outboard of, and clear of stays, lifelines, etc. (like a regular spinnaker, make sure it is outside everything). The canopy will drift slowly to windward until the slack in the anchor rode tightens. The chute will then fill instantly. As this happens, slip the anchor rode out until the boat and para-anchor are on the crest of the wave at the same time. Let out a minimum of 250 feet, then secure it. Do not depend on the bitter end of the rode being secured belowdecks. Double secure it to the bow cleat or anchor windlass. It is important to make sure the anchor rode runs freely through the pennant block without kinking or jamming. A jam up here would put all of the strains onto the pennant line and its fairleads. These are not as strong as the bow fairleads or the larger snatch block on your anchor rode.

20. Watch the bow for a minute to see if it is lying about 50 degrees from the wind. If it is too far from the wind, ease the pennant line forward slowly. If the bow is too close to the wind, take in the pennant line.

21. Adjust the main anchor rode until the chute and boat are on top of their respective waves simultaneously. You will be able to see the chute once it is 200 or even 300 feet away from the boat; even at night it is highly visible through the water, especially as a sea lifts it and the boat.

Properly adjusted, there is less jerking transmitted to the boat.

22. Take a breather now and watch to see how the boat is riding. She should ride quietly in a stable mode, and the bow should fall off only occasionally as it is shoved by a passing roller. The chute and riding sail should quickly pull the bow back up again. If you see the sail luffing slightly as the boat comes close to the crest of the waves, this means you may be too close to the wind. Adjust the pennant lead until the bow is another 5 to 10 degrees off the wind. If the boat continues to head up until the sail luffs, ease the main or trysail sheet slightly, and reduce the lee helm you have tied into the tiller a bit. This will reduce the tendency to head up as quickly.

23. Check for chafe. The most likely place is at the bow snatch block. That is why we have an oversized, 4-inch-diameter roller-bearing sheaved block to use here. The pennant block moves up and down the main line a few inches each time the boat crests over a wave, so chafe has never been a problem for us at this spot.

24. Adjust the main line out 6" to 8" every two hours to spread chafe and wear.

25. As night approaches, set your navigation lights. Carry spare oil lights or battery-operated lights to be sure you always show lights. Although Col-regs say, "Avoid using a strobe light," we feel it is in this situation that we do as stated in Col-regs: "Anything necessary to avoid collision." Therefore, we would use a strobe in severe conditions, just as European fishing boats are legally advised to do while stopped to set or pull in their nets.

26. Get as much rest as possible and put the lee clothes in place or sleep on the cabin sole.

Note: If ever the pennant block should end up right at the bow instead of working as it should, holding the boat at an angle to the seas, return it to position this way. Have your crew standing by at the sheet winch, ready to pull in the pennant line. Quickly ease out about 20 feet of anchor rode while you winch in the pennant line. Secure the main anchor rode again and adjust the pennant until the boat again assumes the proper hove-to position.

Section IV
Other People and Their Stories

Each of the following stories have something to teach about storm management. In each case the crew took positive action to ensure the safety of their boats. The stories range from sailing-ship tales to modern stories. We hope to include other accounts of recent encounters with storms, accounts that show that there is quite often something you can do to improve your situation.

Frank T. Bullen sailed on square-rigged ships during the late 1890s. His ability to describe life afloat is amazing, especially since he ran away to sea an orphan at the age of 12 or 13 to keep from starving on the streets of London. He could not read until a mate on one of the ships he sailed took the time to teach him. His books and short stories eventually made him quite famous. Our favorite is definitely *The Cruise of the Cachalot,* which was reprinted over 30 times. The two excerpts here are taken from a collection of his short stories called, *A Sack of Shakings.* We include them because they not only talk of the slick mentioned throughout this work book, but also show that heaving-to was considered the last chance for big ships, just as we feel it is the best and last chance for small ones.

"A Sea Change"

At the changing of the watch he had her shortened down to the two lower topsails and fore-topmast staysail, and having thus snugged her, went below to snatch, full dressed, a few minutes' sleep. The first moaning breath of the coming gale roused him almost as soon as it reached the ship, and as the watchful Svensen gave his first order, "Lee fore brace!" the skipper appeared at the companion hatch, peering anxiously to windward, where the centre of that gloomy veil seemed to be worn thin. The only light left was just a little segment of blue low down on the eastern horizon, to which, in spite of themselves, the eyes of the travailing watch turned wistfully. But whatever shape the surging thoughts may take in the minds of seamen, the exertion of the moment effectually prevents any development of them into despair in the case of our own countrymen. So, in obedience to the hoarse cries of Mr. Svensen, they strove to get the *Dorothea* into that position where she would be best able to stem

the rising sea, and fore-reach over the hissing sullenness of the long, creaming rollers that, as they came surging past, swept her, a mile at a blow, sideways to leeward leaving a whirling, broadside wake of curling eddies. Silent and anxious, Captain
South hung with one elbow over the edge of the companion, his keen hearing taking note of every complaint made by the trembling timbers beneath his feet, whose querulous voices permeated the deeper note of the storm.

All that his long experience could suggest for the safety of his vessel was put into practice. One by one the scanty show of sail was taken in and secured with extra gasket turns, lest any of them should, showing a loose corner, be ripped adrift by the snarling tempest. By eight bells (4 a.m.) the brig showed nothing to the bleak darkness about but the two gaunt masts, with their ten bare yards tightly braced up against the lee backstays, and the long peaked forefinger of the jib-boom reaching out over the pale foam. A tiny weather-cloth of canvas only a yard square was stopped in the weather main rigging, its small area amply sufficing to keep the brig's head up in the wind.

"The Way of a Ship"

A massive breakwater of two-inch kauri planks was fitted across the deck infront of the saloon for the protection of the afterguard, who dwelt behind it as in a stockaded fort. As the weather grew worse, and the sea got into its gigantic stride, our condition became deplorable; for it was a task of great danger to get from the fo'c'sle to the wheel, impossible to perform without a drenching, and always invested with the risk of being dashed to pieces. We "carried on" recklessly in order to keep her at least ahead of the sea; but at night, when no stars were to be seen, and the compass swung madly through all its thirty-two points, steering was mental and physical torture. In fact, it was only possible to steer at all by the feel of the wind at one's back, and even then the best helmsman among us could not keep her within two points on each side of her course. We lived in hourly expectation of a catastrophe, and for weeks none of us forward ever left off oilskins and sea-boots even to sleep in. At last, on Easter Sunday, three seas swept on board simultaneously. One launched itself like a Niagara over the stern, and one rose on each side in the waist, until the two black hills of water towered above us for fully twenty feet. Then they leaned toward each other and fell, their enormous weight threatening to crush our decks in as if they had been paper. Nothing could be seen of the hull for a smother of white, except for the forecastle-head. When, after what seemed an age, she slowly lifted out of that boiling, yeasty whirl, the breakwater was gone, and so was all the planking of the bulwarks on both sides from poop to forecastle break. Nothing was left but to heave-to, and I, for one, firmly believed that we should never get her up into the wind. However, we were bound to try; and watching the smooth (between two sets of seas), the helm was put hard down and the mizzen hauled out. Round she came swiftly enough, but just as she presented her broadside to the sea, up rose a monstrous wave. Over, over she went—over until the third ratline of the lee rigging was under water; that is to say, the lee rail was full six feet under the sea. One hideous tumult prevailed, one dazzling glare of foaming water surrounded us; but I doubt whether any of us thought of anything but how long we could hold our breath. Had she been less deeply loaded she must have capsized. As it was, she righted again, and came up into the wind still afloat. But never before or since have I seen a vessel behave like that hove-to.

In spite of all these defects in the ship, she reached Lyttelton in safety at last.

From the Drag Device Data Book

(courtesy of Para-Anchors International)

The 75-foot American schooner *Goodjump II* was sailing to Portugal from the U.S. East Coast. The skipper of the boat, Mr. Jeremiah Nixon, had a 28-foot-diameter C-9 military class parachute, converted into a sea anchor.

Goodjump II ran into a storm in mid-Atlantic. The brave senior crew decided to put out the chute, and had some initial difficulty in getting the big canopy in the water; the wind took hold of it on deck and it was almost air-

File S/M-5
Monohull, Steel Schooner
75' x 36 Tons, Full Keel
28-Ft. Diam. Parachute Sea Anchor
Force 9-10 Conditions

~~~~~~

File S/M-5, submitted by Jeremiah Nixon, St. Louis Mo. • Monohull, vessel name "Goodjump II", hailing port St. Louis, steel Schooner, designed by George Suton, LOA 75' x LWL 62' x Beam 15' x Draft 6' 2" x 36 Tons • Full keel • Sea anchor: 28' diameter C-9 military class parachute (Para-Anchors International) on 600' nylon three-strand rode (1" dia.) with 5/8" galvanized swivel • No trip-line • Deployed in deep water during a storm at Latitude 39° 50' N., Longitude 49° 30' W. (mid-Atlantic) with 60 knot winds and seas of about 18' • Vessel's bow stayed snubbed, about 10° to starboard • Drift estimated about 18 n.m. during 18 hours at sea anchor.

~~~~~~

borne. (This problem can be minimized by wetting down the canopy beforehand; nylon cloth is much more manageable and less likely to fly open in the wind when wet and heavy.) The crew persevered, however, and finally had the chute properly deployed on some 600 feet of nylon rode. *Goodjump II* rounded up into the seas, her bow nicely snubbed to her parachute sea anchor, alternately lifting up and then pointing down in 18-foot seas. The following are excerpts from the DDDB feedback submitted by Jeremiah Nixon:

"The para-anchor worked perfectly, we rode nicely. Learned the hard way to deploy it from the windward side of the boat by pushing it right into the water while holding it against the side of the boat. It got loose on our first effort on the lee side and went into the air.

"You asked the question of the angle and movement of our bow during the storm. I cleated the rode to the forward port cleat, and as a result the bow held about 10 degrees to the right of the wind and there was no swing from side to side that I noticed. In fact, the deck was dry and there was no spray or pounding. The 600 feet of rode stretched and raised out of the water at the point of wave crest and then came back down with an easy, controlled feeling.

"We drank beer and ate chili during the worst, and I got a solid 6 hours of sleep at a time when we had to wear a safety harness because of wind, when we went forward to check on chafe.

"No trip-line is necessary. Just motor up to it and bring it up. These are some of the reasons why I consider your equipment the most important safety item on my boat . . . I will never make an ocean passage without one on board. People must realize that ocean cruising can be safe if you go with the idea that you will go into a defensive position before the seas build too high. The flat-out philosophy of professional racers must be disregarded by the small crew cruising yachts."

Two Stories from the June Queen's Birthday Storm

Mary T's Story

In June 1994, over 80 boats were headed north out of New Zealand, the majority of them bound for Tonga as part of a cruising/racing rally. It was late in the season, in fact only two weeks before the official start of winter. Although winds were blowing at 30 knots for almost a week and had delayed the official start of the rally, they were from a favorable direction. Forecasts called for improving conditions, so boats left when they felt ready to do so. Unfortunately, as happens about three or four times a year, a low formed in the tropics and moved south to arrive half way along the fleet's route as an extratropical cyclonic disturbance, its wind strengths increased when it stalled against a ridge of high pressure. Winds recorded by ships in the area confirm those reported here, 60 knots for two days, with gusts to 75. According to the rescue pilots involved during this storm, conditions were as bad as they've seen. It is interesting to note that they never said the conditions were the worst they'd seen, only just as bad—or in other words, people sailing in these areas at these times of the year can encounter winds and seas such as these if luck goes against them. As reported elsewhere, 7 boats were abandoned and 4 lives were lost. But here is what the crew of *Mary T*, a Cheoy Lee Offshore 40 yawl told Tom Linskey of SAIL Magazine after sailing through the storm to arrive safely in Fiji: onboard *Mary T*, Sigmund, 54, and Carol Baardsen, 49, daughter Anna, 16, and crew Lianne Audette, 49.

As the storm overtook them:

Carol: "During the Pacific Maritime Net roll call we heard that Arnold's net (a weather/check-in net out of Rarotonga) had warned of a deepening low. We went west to avoid the southeast quadrant, but then the depression headed right for us. By noon we were running under bare poles, and taking a lot of water on board."

(Eventually they discovered that the water was coming in through the cockpit seat lockers and cockpit sole, the hull was sound.)

"When the water reached the floorboards and we weren't staying ahead of it with our cockpit bilge pumps, we put in a PAN call to KeriKeri Radio, giving them our position in case things got worse. By this time the wind was up to about 60 knots, where it stayed for the next two days. The waves were spreader height; every once in a while a combination would come through that was closer to the mast top. The wave tops were blowing off, but not breaking, at least where we were.

"We were at roughly 28 South, 179 East. Quartermaster (the boat that sunk with her three crew) was 60 to 100 miles from us. We heard KeriKeri talking to them; they had a small drogue out but were still doing 6 knots. KeriKeri told them to slow down more, and that stimulated us to slow our boat down."

About their improvised drogue:

Carol: "First we put out a 300' length of 3/4" nylon in a bight (one end secured to each quarter of the boat, so that they were dragging a loop) that slowed us down from 9 knots to 6, but we were still going too fast. Sigmund tried putting out a sheet with our dinghy anchor and old mizzen on it (we'd bought new sails in New Zealand) and that slowed us down another half knot.

"We didn't have a drogue onboard, but Sigmund is a master at improvisation. To the swivel on our stern anchor line, which is 300' of 1" nylon with 60' of chain, he shackled the tack of our old mainsail. (Cruiser Pete Sutter, a San Francisco sailmaker, had asked us to take it up to the villagers of Rambi Island, in Vanua Levu, Fiji, who were building a boat.) This assemblage went off our weather quarter and down at about a 45 degree angle, at right angles to the boat, and kept us lying ahull.

"We tried leading it off the bow but that was a disaster; lots of water coming aboard, the boat uncomfortable, so we led it back off the stern quarter. We rolled, but we never rolled over, probably due to the traditional hull form: a full length keel and cutaway forefoot. Once we got the drogue out, we realized that the steering had broken. We put on the emergency tiller and lashed it hard over."

(After the storm passed, Sigmund dived and lashed the rudder in the center with line, and they used their HydraVane, a self- steerer with an external rudder—which had carried away, but they fitted their spare rudder—and sailed up to Fiji.)

"We feel, in retrospect, like we did fine. That is not to say we were not really scared, especially when the water was up to the floor-boards. We kept two-hour bilge watches, with everybody else in their bunks. Except for the steering, and the shredded dodger and weather cloths, we had no damage.

[Why does Carol think other boats, like *Destiny,* came to grief?] "It could have been a matter of bad luck. Why did a [modern] Norse-man 447 have that happen, and not us? They were running off, and if you're running you can broach and roll, which sounds like what happened. With our boat, which surfs like a brick, warps were a much better option.

"But everybody did different things. We've talked to quite a few boats up here who did run off, and were just fine. *Exotic Escort,* a Davidson 45 with a delivery crew of four tough young Kiwi blokes, just trucked along, having several 200-mile days in a row. But I'm 49, Sigmund is 54, Lianne is 49, and Anna, although a large healthy 16, was seasick, so we didn't feel like it was our option to run off and steer for days on end. If you run off with only one person able to steer the boat they're going to get tired, and make mistakes. *Flying Cloud II,* a New Zealand boat, were in the worst of it, and their autopilot steered them, running off through most of it.

As the storm overtook them: Sigmund: "Trying to cross in front of the depression, we did 86 miles during the hours of darkness, a screaming sail through the night, but then we figured out that 300 miles out from the center it was blowing 60 knots. There was no way we could go over, under or around the thing, and we were just going to have to take a licking.

"We started running off under bare poles, doing 8s and 9s, surging to an occasional 10. The boat was comfortable, we felt safe, we felt in control, but the seas were big enough that there was the possibility of broaching, and getting rolled or pitchpoled. We thought: do we want to broach or roll at 8 or 9 knots.

About their mainsail drogue:

OTHER PEOPLE AND THEIR STORIES

"Once the drogue was out we were lying beam on, which was a little scary, but some interesting things happened. The keel stalled completely, and we made a slick to windward. We were sideslipping, pointing west but moving north, sliding off at about 1.2 knots. The boat heeled over, presenting the turn of the bilge to the waves. Though they'd still hit us with a hell of a smash, we were fading from the punch, so they didn't hit quite as hard. The drogue helped dampen the motion of the boat, too, and our low moment of inertia may have helped steady us."*

"If we'd led the drogue directly from the stern, the boat would probably have lain the same way, 90 degrees to the waves. Nothing was going to pull the bow off. Should we have put up a scrap of sail forward? I don't think the gear or the sail could have stood it, and we would have ended up busting something or hurting someone."

"Two people on Barient 32s couldn't budge the drogue; there was that much strain on it. It took three days before we could get it in!"

What worked for them, and what they'd recommend: Early, early on, Carol cooked a big pot of rice, so we had food. We took everything off the deck and stowed it below. Using earplugs let us get some rest. Ski goggles: essential for work on deck, better than diving masks. Space blankets—we had hail!—and polar plus blankets: even when wet they were warm. A manual bilge pump belowdecks; there comes a point when it's unsafe to be on deck. We'd love to have a big Edson below. A 406 EPIRB; we didn't have one, but now we have one on order.

About doing what you have to do: "Afterward, the skipper of the HMNZS *Monowai* told me, 'I did everything I knew how to do, and then I started doing what I had to do.'"

"It doesn't take very long before the textbooks go out the window, and you're down to experimenting, like trying the drogue off the bow or off the stern. You do what you have to do. We used our Lavac head for pumping. We took a piece of hose, jammed it in, packed it with rags, and pumped. At one point, alarmed that our bow wouldn't fall off and thinking it might be the windage of the mizzen, I figured, what the hell, let's get rid of the mizzen and drag that behind us, too, so we can get the stern up into the wind.

"We were very high when we got to Fiji—that happens at the end of every tough passage. When the waves started going down, I found, to my surprise, regret. I was going to see this only once in a my life and never again, and there was a kind of regret. We read about mountainous waves, and without any hyperbole these looked like great

---

*In later correspondence with the Baardsens, we learned that their sea anchor, improvised from an old sail and swivel, was acting more like a drogue. As it was attached at only one point, it was not gripping much water and, in fact, hung down at a 45-degree angle from the boat. In Section III there is a discussion of the reasons a boat may lie beam-on to the wind with a para-anchor set. The same information would probably hold true in this case.

ranges of mountains, with snow on top. They were fantastic. They were so beautiful."

Sigmund and Carol Baardson sent a detailed letter about other aspects of their storm preparations which they asked us to share with readers. Sigmund has been sailing since he was eight years old. He has worked as a delivery skipper, charter skipper, sailing teacher and has cruised on Mary T for four years now. Carol, his wife and Anna, his daughter, have sailed with Sigmund all during the past 16 years. Their crew, Lianne Audette, has a lot of racing experience on larger boats, the Big Boat series in San Francisco, Mexican ocean races, plus assorted deliveries. Yet Sigmund rates the experience level of his crew and himself as only 'long on years, light on depth.'
Several of the observations in their letter are well worth considering. (I do not include those already recorded by Tom Linskey on the previous pages). I repeat them here, point by point and in the order written by the Baardsen's:

1. Life raft lashed in cradle on foredeck—wrong place for liferaft. Liferaft will be shifted aft into our cockpit to reduce volume. Cockpit volume—foot well = one cubic meter or 2000 pounds total weight of water. Cockpit volume including footwell—two cubic meters equal to 4,000 pounds of water.

2. Two manual bilge pumps on deck, one in seat locker. NO GOOD! Too uncomfortable and dangerous to pump on deck. Both the electric bilge pumps failed due to water on the electrical panel and not due to rubbish in bilge or blockage (the most commonly sited reason for bilge pump failure).

3. Error—trying to avoid storm—impossible, waste of time and energy. First, there were 60 knots of wind, 300 miles out from the center. That's an area from San Francisco to Ensenada. Secondly, weather predictions were delayed, inaccurate and often in conflict, Fiji vs. Auckland.

4. Good—we started preparations early. Hurricane Raymond in Mexico taught us that hurricanes are preceded by outlying squalls and rain that interfere with preparations. It also taught us that met office reports are sometimes late—as much as 8 or 12 hours and storm positions can be in error by over 100 miles. The U.S. met services reported the storm's rate of travel at 4 knots, actual rate of travel was 18-20 knots. Australian met service says any cyclone path predictions have an average accuracy of 200 kilometers. Therefore it pays to start preparations early.

5. Error—I had a list of preparations in my mind; close nonessential through-hulls, double-lash gear, plot D.R. charge batteries, etc. But it was all in my mind. It was not written out and posted for the rest of the crew to examine and memorize at leisure. I had it memorized but that didn't help them.

6. Bad—upon receipt of storms reports, I started preparations before plotting the storm position and predicted course. As I expected it to be upon us in four hours or less, I started preparations instead of sitting down for a few minutes to discuss the larger picture with the crew. These people are experienced and good. This failure had a bad effect on morale.

In anticipation, the anxiety level was very high. Once it started to blow, everything was okay—we had a plan and we had challenges to occupy us. The possibility of sinking was a real and concrete problem, fear was not. We were all too busy to be afraid.

7. Bad error—you can always tell the California and USA boats by all the junk on deck. I waited too long before jettisoning jerry cans and never did jettison the sailboard. Result, unnecessary hazard to the crew and broken lifeline stanions.

8. Error—failed to issue seasick pills, lost effectiveness of one crew member.

9. Good—ran engine periodically to keep batteries topped up and engine warm and dry for easy restart. Checked engine for flooding prior to each start-up. Elevated crankcase oil level. Drained exhaust line and water pot (water lift). Turned engine over by hand first to feel for water in cyclinders or exhaust manifold. Starting a flooded engine results in bent rods.

10. Good—food; we used baked potatoes. Baked in the oven they are safe and easy to cook. They keep your pockets and hands warm, plus are easily vomited, to say nothing of good food and energy value. We also used rice in pressure cooker.

11. Bad—tea, hot chocolate and coffee interfere with sleep.

12. Error—side curtains (spray cloths). Our brand new Sunbrella spray curtains in the lifelines blew to bits. The streaming ends snapping in the wind were a hazard to the helmsman. They could have put out an eye or flicked off an ear. We had to cut them away.

13. Error—dodger, waited too long to remove it. It started to pull its hardware out of the deck.

14. Good—once removed, we lashed the dodger frame longitudinally in the cabin to divide the cabin and reduce the fall hazard.

15. Good—sail bags on cabin sole reduced slip hazard, reduced fall hazard, provided sleeping space. (Note: Carol and Sigmund disagree slightly only on this one point—Carol feeling the sail bags added a tripping hazard that might have been potentially more dangerous than the slipping hazard.)

16. Good—filled all lamps early. Kerosene lamps provide cheery light, non-blinding, non-electrical.

17. Good—for comfort, talcum powder on the whole body before getting into the bunk to dry skin.

18. Good—comfort—space blankets were great on top of wet mattresses.

19. Good—high quality foulies with built-in harness. Working on deck even for the briefest periods we wore shoes, harness and foulie tops. Even in warm water, hypothermia is a real danger because you may be stuck on deck longer than anticipated, plus the wind chill, plus the stinging spray. Starkers (nude) is not on for working on deck, even if it is commonly done to save time.

20. Good—on returning below we dry off with the artificial auto wash chamois. Towels waste space, water, laundry and time.

21. Good—vaseline on feet prevents 'immersion feet.'

22. Good—our jacklines are mountain climbers (flat) webbing. Unlike wire, it doesn't roll underfoot.

23. Good—safety—we used masthead strobe as we were not under command (underweigh) and it save batteries. Running lights would not have been appropriate.

24. Good—Big RACOR filter had no problem in spite of three liters of water getting into fuel tanks through the tank vents.

25. Bad—unused halyard beat hell out of painted wood mast.

We thank Sigmund and Carol for being extremely candid in their responses to our questions, but we do feel they have underrated their own reactions to the storm. Though things did not go perfectly, they kept working as a team, taking care of the boat and the crew. They came through with only limited gear damage. We hope their insights will encourage other people to help us further expand this handbook with information about how they successfully weathered severe gales and storms, and what lessons they learned.

Peter O'Neill's Story

Although Peter O'Neill suffered both the loss of his boat and a broken shoulder, during the storm off New Zealand in June of '94, his discussion of how he stabilized the situation shows an excellent example of jury-rigging a para-anchor and riding sail to heave-to.

Report on Voyage of *Silver Shadow,* by Peter O'Neill, owner, *Silver Shadow* NZ4520, as told to Tom Linskey:

"Kerikeri Radio confirmed the low was approaching our area but nobody realized the speed the low was moving or the increasing intensity. The barometer had dropped from 1018 to 1004 at that time. By 2400 on 4/06/94, the barometer had dropped to 997. At 1500, we changed to a storm jib and put three reefs in the main. We were still running quite comfortably. At 1700, we dropped the main and continued under storm jib with winds rising to 50 knots. Our boat speed was 8-8.5 knots. No problems. At 0230-0300 on 5/06/95, without any warning, we were knocked down to approximately 160 degrees by a huge breaking wave. The wave came at 30 degrees approximate to the prevailing seas and struck us on the port side. We were running with the wind and seas at the time. We lost our mast in the first knockdown. Our position was approximately 29.55S 179.1W.

We had the washboards tied in place but some water came in through the gaps. We assessed the situation—rig down, dodger down, radar tower on transom half down, no water coming in, SSB did not work, aerial in backstay. Action: bolt cutters—two crew took an hour to cut away the rig. No damage to hull. Spare SSB was erected on backstay but SSB still not working. Water must have got in during our knockdown. Manual portable whale bilge pump (large) was used to clear the water—took only 10 minutes. Great equipment.

At one stage during this, water was gushing in under the floorboards near the mast. We thought we had been holed by the broken mast. On inspection, we found the speed transducer had been pushed out. With some relief, this was secured back in place. We had wooden bungs in case this did not work. We then assessed our situation. No hull damage, no water coming in, mast down. We would jury-rig in the morning and sail on. The yacht was comfortably lying ahull, no evidence of breaking seas visible. It was too risky to stay on deck longer than necessary so any further action delayed until daylight.

At approximately 0300 on 5/06/94, another breaking wave hit us and rolled us 360 degrees. The floorboards came up and I finished with my head and shoulders in the bilges, so I could not move. We were now being knocked frequently past 90 degrees. We must put out drogues to bring the boat around to the waves. It was blowing 70 knots!

We used #4 jib, tying the clews and with difficulty in the conditions, this was tied to transom on 200 meters of line. It was working but not sufficiently. Arranged to tie the drogue off the bow. Erected a jockey pole on the pushpit (transom) and rigged the trysail along the port lifelines. The wind on the trysail and the drogue off the bow helped to keep us at a better angle to the seas. Crew administered painkillers to me. We discussed our situation. The life raft had been ripped from the deck during our 360. Our SSB was out but all other electricals were working—including our GPS and VHF. Emergency aerial for VHF was attached. We decided that we did not have sufficient diesel to motor to Tonga. With no life raft, no SSB, and an injured crew—the extent of which we could only guess—we activated the EPIRB (we had two EPIRBs).

We taped a strobe light to a winch handle on the cabintop, which was picked up by the Hercules when they came over at first light. They flew over twice at a low level in terrible conditions. We used our VHF with auxiliary aerial and could communicate with them. They said they could not copy us and asked us to reply with one click for 'yes' and two clicks for 'no' to their questions. This we did. They informed us there were many EPIRBs activated in our area. We said we were okay, they said they would contact us later.

We continued to ride out the storm. Approximately 1400, an Orion flew over and we communicated with them with no problem. They asked us about our life raft as one had been sighted—orange canopy, black base—but no EPIRB (two were aboard *Silver Shadow*). They were looking for other yachts and said rescue ships were on their way but would not reach us until tomorrow. They wanted to assess our situation: 1-5, 5 being we were in need of urgent rescue. *Silver Shadow* was not taking in water, I had been stabilized with plenty of painkillers, so we believed we were safe for the time being. After discussion, we said a 2, knowing others were in trouble. The Orion said they would see us tomorrow.

That night was the longest of our lives. The storm continued. We couldn't think of anything further we could do to stabilize the boat. We had to sit it out.

We had lashed the wheel over but with the continuing bashing, part of the steering inside the boat had been ripped away. We had auxiliary steering but considered our position—no life raft, no SSB emergency steering, only enough fuel for three days motoring, and some of our emergency fuel tied to the deck had been lost. We wanted to know if we could be towed, but this was unlikely due to the size of the seas.

OTHER PEOPLE AND THEIR STORIES

We had to make ready to abandon *Silver Shadow*—a hard decision.

The Monowai said they couldn't entertain towing *Silver Shadow* in the seas as they had other yachts to search for.

The bravery and skill of the crew on the Monowai was of the highest order. The Captain and crew cared for us over the next four days as they searched for other yachts. Their hospitality was excellent and helped tremendously in our recovery. On return to New Zealand, we learned of the tremendous efforts of the search and rescue team at Lower Hutt. We commend them for their skills and the way they kept our families and friends informed during our ordeal. We thank everyone involved in our rescue and hope they will receive the recognition they deserve."

***

In later telephone conversations with Peter, we learned he has many years of racing experience in Wellington, New Zealand, an area known for stormy sailing. He has often hove-to to ride out fronts in the Tasman Sea. Peter chose to run during this situation as HAM radio reports, based on delayed and unfortunately inaccurate forecasts, said the track of the storm was such that by running with the wind, it could be avoided. His words to me were almost an exact parallel to those written about 100 years ago by Captain Voss and quoted at the beginning of this handbook. Peter said: 'We were running along quite well when, suddenly, without any warning we were knocked down to approximately 160 degrees by a huge breaking wave.'

Peter and his crew showed seamanship of the highest order, stabilizing the situation and getting the boat into a safe, hove-to situation, then making the decision to delay their rescue until others in more difficult situations were assisted. Since returning to New Zealand Peter has worked with yachting authorities to further assess the problems encountered in this storm. Six months after the incident his shoulder is almost back to full usage.

Section V
Storm Trysail and Storm Trysail Track Installation

"A trysail is a most seamanlike storm sail"
—Jeremy Howard-Williams, author, *Sails*

This is the sail for those who like to be prepared. It is one required by offshore racing rules, and is just as important for people who journey across oceans on cruising boats. Since it is heavily built, it can take over when conditions threaten to split your deeply reefed mainsail. Since it can be used boomless it can fill the bill when your boom is damaged or broken.

This is a very basic sail, lean and tough with no extras; no battons, no headboard. As your strongest small sail it is the ultimate in reliability. If you spend any time offshore there will be a reason to use it, be it to beat off a lee shore, to lay hove-to in the classic position, or as a riding sail when you are forced to lay to a sea-anchor.

Since sailors are, by nature, optimistic, I believe some long forgotten seaman said, "Let's give it a try," thus naming this tough little sail the "trysail."

The following diagrams should help you to build and install a trysail for any type of sailing boat, modern racing sloop, classic cruising hull. or even gaff-rigged old timer.

Two Classic Trysail Designs

Trysail A
Cross cut
as used on Taleisin

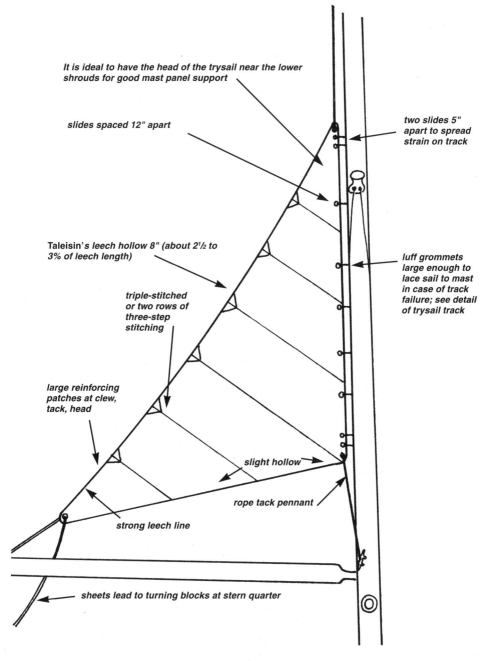

It is ideal to have the head of the trysail near the lower shrouds for good mast panel support

slides spaced 12" apart

two slides 5" apart to spread strain on track

Taleisin's leech hollow 8" (about 2½ to 3% of leech length)

luff grommets large enough to lace sail to mast in case of track failure; see detail of trysail track

triple-stitched or two rows of three-step stitching

large reinforcing patches at clew, tack, head

slight hollow

rope tack pennant

strong leech line

sheets lead to turning blocks at stern quarter

The two slides at the head of the trysail help spread the strain along the sail track

The adjustment for the heavy-duty leech line is easily reached in its position at the trysail clew

Trysail B
Mitre cut

This sail is harder to build and more costly than Trysail A. This cut is recommended by Ted Hood, Sr.

The leech seams can be reinforced with flutter patches (triangles) to strengthen this high-load area

Normal Dacron sail cloth stretches least in this direction

Leech can be made with either a folded tabling or Dacron tape

Cloth should be about 2 ounces heavier than mainsail. Taleisin's trysail is "storm orange" 9-ounce Dacron, available from Bainbridge

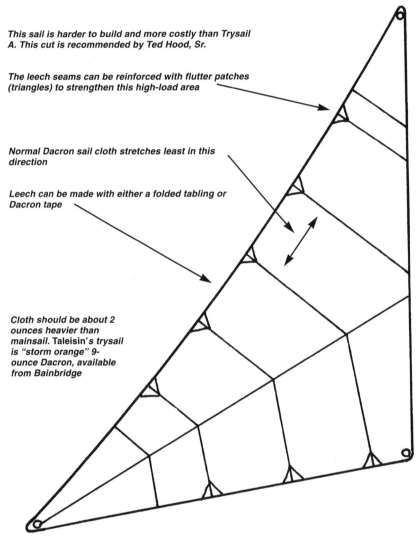

If the trysail is cut with the panels parallel to the leech (leech cut), lengthwise stretch could cause the leech to hook and possibly flog. Flogging can quickly cause premature cloth failure. Some sailmakers prefer a leech-cut trysail, as this design eliminates the chance of stitched seams' separating

Notice the hollow in the trysail leech. This is important, as it reduces flogging (fluttering). There is also no headboard or battens; the reef points could be tied around the luff rope if a smaller riding sail is required when hove-to. To date this reef has not been needed

Trysail C
Two Modern High-Aspect Trysails

Trysails C and D represent the latest thinking from two major sailmakers. Although at first glance they look like heavily reefed mainsails, there are important differences. The sails are designed to be set loose-footed for two reasons. First, water from breaking waves can run off without stressing the foot of the sails or the boom. Second, the tack is raised sufficiently to clear the furled mainsail. Both sails are also designed so they can be used with the clew attached to the boom or sheeted to a turning block on the quarter of the boat, just like a jib. My impression is that these high-aspect sails are what could be called "performance trysails," ideally suited to very short keeled boats. They would work well as a substitute for a fourth reef in the mainsail for driving to windward in storm conditions. At the same time, with their shorter foot they would have less tendency to drive a properly hove-to, short-keeled hull up into the wind, where it could tack inadvertently

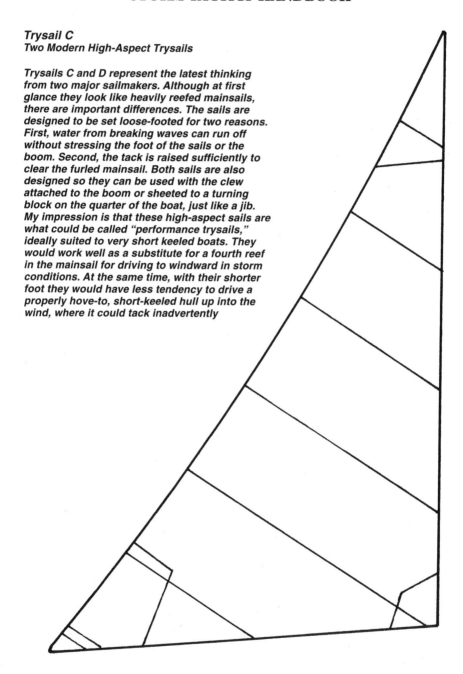

Courtesy of North Sails, Mark Baxter, Designer

STORM TRYSAIL INSTALLATION

Trysail D

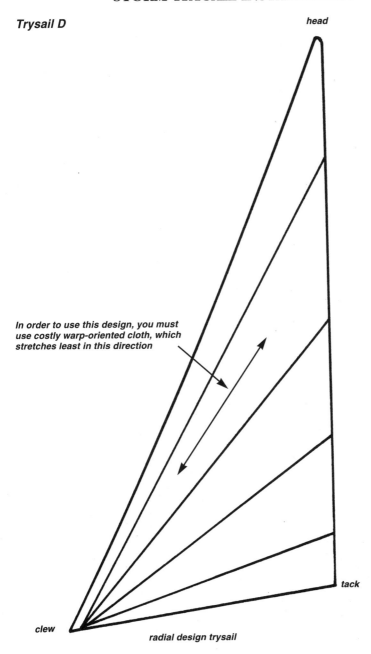

head

In order to use this design, you must use costly warp-oriented cloth, which stretches least in this direction

tack

clew

radial design trysail

Courtesy of Hood Sails, Dave Simmons, Designer

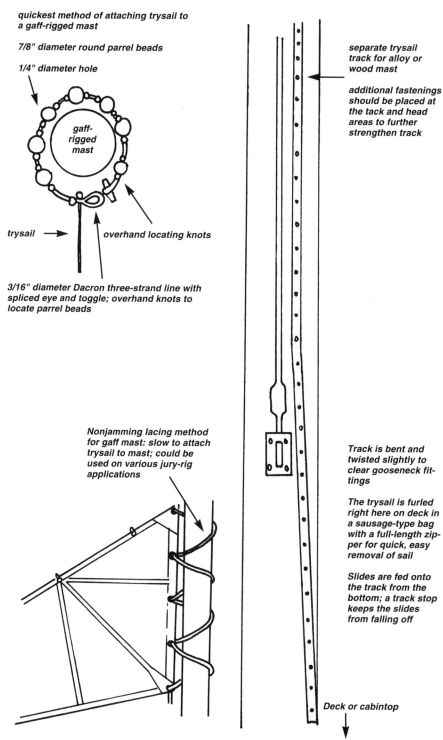

quickest method of attaching trysail to a gaff-rigged mast

7/8" diameter round parrel beads

1/4" diameter hole

gaff-rigged mast

trysail → *overhand locating knots*

3/16" diameter Dacron three-strand line with spliced eye and toggle; overhand knots to locate parrel beads

Nonjamming lacing method for gaff mast: slow to attach trysail to mast; could be used on various jury-rig applications

separate trysail track for alloy or wood mast

additional fastenings should be placed at the tack and head areas to further strengthen track

Track is bent and twisted slightly to clear gooseneck fittings

The trysail is furled right here on deck in a sausage-type bag with a full-length zipper for quick, easy removal of sail

Slides are fed onto the track from the bottom; a track stop keeps the slides from falling off

Deck or cabintop

STORM TRYSAIL INSTALLATION

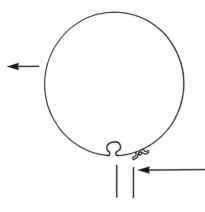

Track fasteners for alloy spars: use machine screws if wall thickness of mast is 1/8" or more; if thinner, use rivets

Grade 40 monel rivets 3/16" diameter (1,000 lbs. tensile strength) or Grade 51 all stainless-steel rivets (1,200 lbs.)

For wood mast: silicon bronze wood screws

Trysail track 1 1/4" away from mainsail track or enough to clear mainsail slides, etc.

This round thimble, which is sewn onto the sail's bolt rope, provides a universal-type movement that helps reduce slide friction when lowering or raising the sail. Slides that are attached with nylon tubular webbing tend to jam a bit when raising or lowering

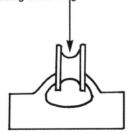

External sail slides have less friction than internal slug slides

A track riser may be necessary for slides to clear various pieces of mast hardware. A riser also is usually used full length on a wood spar so that the slides do not scratch the mast finish

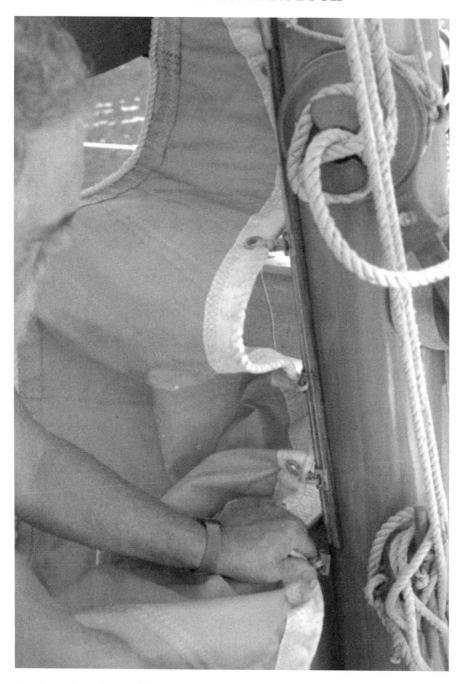

The trysail track should be on the starboard side of the main track. This puts it next to the main halyard winch (shown above). Switching halyard and hoisting sail are easier this way

The 96-square-foot trysail we used on Taleisin *is 33% (the size rec-ommended by the Offshore Racing Council) of the mainsail area. Rod Stephens and Ted Hood, Sr., recommend a smaller trysail, 25% of mainsail area. But we have carried this one in winds of 89 knots with no problems*

The Storm Trysail

This sail generally lives in a bag hidden at the bottom of the sail lock-er, only to be seen in a storm; it should be brought to the surface well before it is needed. The time to try it out is in a marina; anyone who saw a seamanlike skipper checking the sheet leads and tack position of a trysail in Cowes before the 1979 Fastnet race may have laughed. They won't anymore.—Rob James, Author, *Ocean Sailing*

Appendix

From the *American Practical Navigator,* by Bowditch (1938 edition)
We include this section because it has a particularly interesting discussion of handling a vessel in the storm area. It is important to know where your boat actually lies when and if you are caught in a cyclone or in a sub-tropical cyclone. Is the storm center to the east of you, the west? Is there some tactic you could choose to avoid the center? This is all well described by Nathaniel Bowditch. If you find the first few pages, which describe how storms form, to be slow reading, please skip them and begin your study at the section called: Handling your vessel within the storm area. What follows is 'must know' information for ocean voyagers.

We have taken these pages from the 1938 edition of Bowditch rather than a more recent edition because this U.S. Hydrographic Office publication is constantly being updated for commercial seamen. Therefore, items of interest to sailors and those cruising under sail (even with auxiliary engines) are given less attention now that almost all commercial shipping is done without sail.

CHAPTER XXII
CYCLONIC STORMS

Variations of atmospheric pressure.—The prevailing distribution of atmospheric pressure previously described (chap. XXI) and the attendant circulation of the winds are those which become evident after the effects of many disturbing causes have been eliminated by the process of averaging observations covering an extended period of time. However, conditions over the globe do not always conform to these averages. On some days pressure and winds may be distributed much as they appear on a chart of averages. More frequently, however, the actual conditions in various localities lie to one side or the other of the averages, and it is sometimes difficult to distinguish the features which the averages bring out.

Confining our attention for the time being to the subject of atmospheric pressure, it may be said that this, at any given point on the earth's surface, is in a constant state of change, the mercurial barometer rarely becoming stationary, and then only for a few hours in succession. The variations which the pressure undergoes may be divided into two classes, viz, periodic, or those which are continuously in operation, repeating themselves within fixed intervals of time, long or short; and nonperiodic or accidental, which occur irregularly, and are of varying duration and extent.

Periodic variations.—Of the periodic class of changes the most important are the seasonal, which have been already to some extent described, and the diurnal. The latter consists of the daily occurrence of two barometric maxima, or points of highest pressure, with two intervening minima. Under ordinary circumstances, with the atmosphere free from disturbances, the barometer each day attains its first minimum about 4 a.m. As the day advances

143

the pressure increases, and a maximum, or point of greatest pressure, is reached about 10 a.m. From this time the mercury again rises, reaching its second maximum about 10 p.m. The range of this diurnal oscillation is greatest at the equator, where it amounts to about ten hundredths (0.10) of an inch. It diminishes with increased latitude, and near the poles it seems to vanish entirely. In middle latitudes it is much more apparent in summer than in winter.

Nonperiodic variations.—The equatorial slope of the belt of high pressure which encircles the globe in either hemisphere near latitudes 30° to 35° is characterized by the marked uniformity of its meteorological conditions, the temperature, wind, and weather changes proper to any given season repeating themselves as day succeeds day with almost monotonous regularity. Here the diurnal oscillation of the barometer constitutes the main variation to which the atmospheric pressure is subjected. On the polar slope of these belts conditions are very different, the elements which go to make up the daily weather here passing from phase to phase without regularity, with the result that no two days are precisely alike; and as regards atmospheric pressure, it may be said that in marked contrast with the uniformity of the torrid zone, the barometer in the temperate zone is constantly subjected to nonperiodic or accidental fluctuations of such extent that the periodic diurnal variation is scarcely apparent, the mercurial barometer at a given station frequently rising or falling several tenths of an inch in 24 hours.

The explanation of this rapid change of conditions in the higher latitudes is found in the approach and passage of extensive areas of alternately high and low pressure, which affect alike, although to a different degree, all the barometers coming within their scope. The general direction of motion of these areas is that of the prevailing winds. In the latitudes which are under consideration, therefore, their movement is in general from west to east though often with a large north or south component.

Cyclonic and anticyclonic circulations.—A central area of low pressure is surrounded by a system of winds which exhibit a tendency to draw in toward the center but at the same time circulate about it; the direction of this circulation being in the Northern Hemisphere opposite to the motion of the hands of a watch. A rotation of this kind is defined as 'cyclonic' rotation, and the area of low pressure is termed a 'cyclone.' In the Southern Hemisphere cyclonic rotation is directed in the opposite sense, that is, with the motion of the hands of a watch.

Around the center of an area of high pressure a similar system of winds will be found, but blowing in the reverse direction. Here the barometric gradients are directed radially outward, with the result that in place of an inflow we have an outflow, the circulatory motion being right handed or with the hands of a watch in the Northern Hemisphere, left handed or against the hands of a watch in the Southern.

APPENDIX

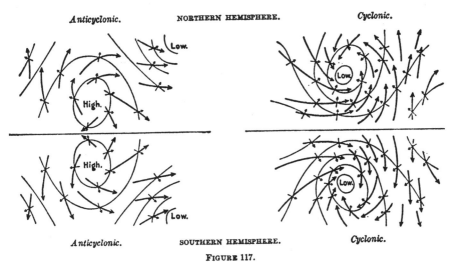

Anticyclonic.   NORTHERN HEMISPHERE.   *Cyclonic.*

Anticyclonic.   SOUTHERN HEMISPHERE.   *Cyclonic.*

FIGURE 117.

The light arrows show the direction of the gradients; the heavy arrows the direction of the winds.

A rotation of this kind is said to be "anticyclonic," and the area of high pressure is termed an "anticyclone."

All these features are shown in the accompanying diagram (fig. 117), which exhibits the general character of cyclonic (around a low) and anticyclonic (around a high) circulations in the Northern and Southern Hemispheres, respectively. The closed curves represent the isobars, or lines along which the barometric pressure is the same; the short arrows show the direction of the gradients, which are everywhere at right angles to the isobars; the long arrows give the directions of the winds, deflected by the earth's rotation to the right of the gradients in the Northern Hemisphere, to the left in the Southern.

Features of cyclonic and anticyclonic regions.—Certain features of the two areas may here by contrasted. In the anticyclonic, the successive isobars are as a rule far apart, showing weak gradients and consequently light winds. In the cyclonic area, on the other hand, the successive isobars are usually crowded together, showing steep gradients and strong winds.

The anticyclonic area is a region of outflowing winds, as shown in figure 117. The divergence of the wind streams at sea level necessitates a compensating downward flow of air from aloft. Since descending air is compressed and consequently is heated, a condition favoring the dissipation of clouds results. The cyclonic area, however, is a region of inflowing winds. The convergence of the winds at sea level demands that there be a general tendency for an upward movement of air. Since ascending air expands and consequently cools, the formation of clouds and precipitation is favored. These considerations explain why in general the approach and presence of anticyclonic areas are in most cases attended by fair weather, although they are not infrequently characterized by scattered showers, whereas the progress of cyclonic areas is usually accompanied by thickly overcast skies, more or less continuous rain, and the generally foul weather which characterizes the ordinary storm at sea.

145

Classification of cyclones.—Cyclones have been classified in various ways. According to duration they are known as semipermanent and migratory; according to season of occurrence, as winter and summer; or according to zone of origin, as topical and extratopical.

There are several semipermanent cyclones in different parts of the world, the most prominent of which are, in the Northern Hemisphere, the so-called Icelandic and Aleutian lows, and in the Southern Hemisphere those of Ross Sea and Weddell Sea. The Aleutian low is active during winter only.

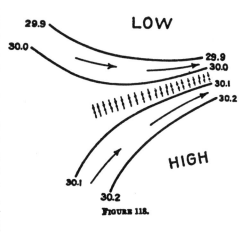

Figure 118.

The regions occupied by the semipermanent cyclones constitute what may be called the 'graveyards' of the migratory cyclones. Many of the traveling cyclones move directly into these areas, merging with and reinforcing the semipermanent cyclones, and at the same time losing their own identity. In fact it may be said that the semipermanent cyclones are maintained largely by the tendency for the migratory ones, after they have attained their maximum intensity, to collect in certain favored regions, where they often come virtually to a standstill. The areas so favored are zones where the thermal differences between the polar regions and the relatively warm open oceans are sharply concentrated. Such a condition in itself leads to the development and perpetuation of a cyclonic circulation with attendant low pressure.

The two general types of migratory cyclonic storms, known as tropical and extratropical, though chiefly distinguished from one another by the zone of origin, also differ from one another in size, structure, intensity, direction of movement, the distribution of temperature and rainfall within the storm area, and the way in which they are maintained or dissipated. Storms of the latter class—that is, extratropical—are by far the more numerous, being of daily occurrence in middle and northern latitudes. Their number, as well as intensity, is greater, however, in the colder seasons of the year. Their place of origin is not restricted and they may and do form over the continents, though in much larger numbers over the oceans. Generally, but not always, they increase in intensity on passing from the continents to the oceans and diminish in energy on passing from the oceans to the continents.

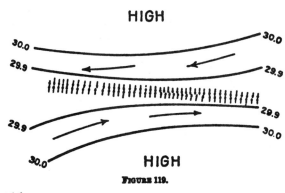

Figure 119.

APPENDIX

Formation and development of extratropical cyclones.—The great majority of extratropical cyclones do not form haphazardly within the circulation of the prevailing westerlies but at special points where a convergence of wind streams occurs. Two types of pressure distribution favoring convergence are shown in figures 118 and 119. In one case the air currents are flowing almost in the same direction; in the other they flow in almost opposite directions. the bringing-together of air currents which have originated in widely separated regions and which consequently possess differing properties leads to the development of a comparatively narrow zone, generally less than 100 miles in width, in which there is a rapid transition of temperature from one air current or 'air mass' to the other. The formation of such a zone or 'front,' as it is termed, is the prelude to the development of an extratropical cyclone.

This preliminary stage is shown in figure 120. Here the converging of two distinct air currents, both of which are flowing towards the east has concentrated the temperature and density differences in a narrow zone represented by the heavy dashed line. The air current to the north of the front is relatively cold and dry, being characteristically of polar or sub-polar origin,

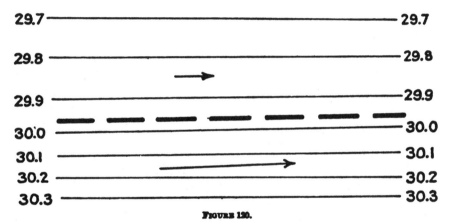

FIGURE 120.

and it is moving comparatively slowly, as indicated by the widely separated isobars. On the other hand, that to the south of the front is relatively warm and moist being characteristically of tropical or sub-tropical origin, and it is moving comparatively rapidly as indicated by the closely spaced isobars. The boundary between the air masses is not vertical. On the contrary, because of the density differences between the air masses, the frontal surface assumes a gentle slope (on the order of 1/100), the polar air lying under the tropical air in the form of a thin wedge.

The next stage is the development of cyclonic rotation at some point along the boundary. This tends to distort the front and cause it to exhibit a wave-like corrugation, as illustrated in figure 121. Occasionally further intensification of the cyclonic rotation fails to take place, and the wave travels rapidly along the front in an easterly direction, at the same time maintaining its flat character. Almost invariably, however, the cyclonic rotation, once it has been concentrated, intensifies progressively. This leads to a closed circulation with accompanying closed isobars and increased barometric gradients. The origi-

147

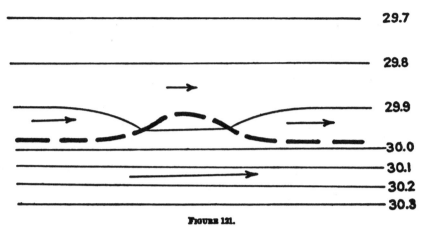

FIGURE 121.

nally flat wave becomes more pronounced, and a center of low pressure appears at its crest. This stage is illustrated in figure 122.

The cyclones thus formed at a front have at first an oblong shape.

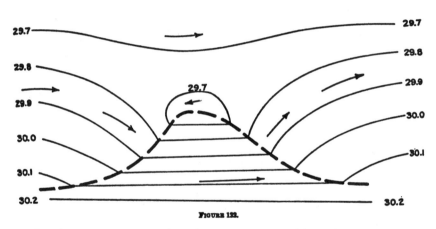

FIGURE 122.

Later they become more circular. They intensify quickly and move rapidly. As they intensify, the increasing circulation around the center tends to fold up the front and consequently to narrow the tongue of warm air, which is termed the 'warm sector' of the cyclone. The air within the warm sector is raised from the ground, whence it flows away above the body of cold air which lies ahead of the wave. Eventually the front is doubled up on itself, and the center of low pressure is completely surrounded at the ground by the cold air. When this stage has been reached the cyclone is said to be 'occluded.' It now begins to resemble more and more a circular vortex and to lose intensity. Thereafter it gradually fills up and disappears, merges with a semi-permanent system, or is absorbed by a newer and more vigorous cyclone which has developed at some other point on the front. A partly occluded cyclone is shown in figure 123.

The ascent of the air in the warm sector and its replacement at the surface by the cold air constitutes a process which is continually furnishing kinetic energy to the cyclonic system. The resulting gain of energy is mani-

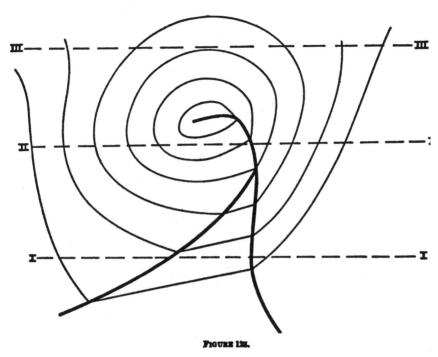

III — III

II — II

I — I

FIGURE 123.

fested by the increasing strength of the circulation as the cyclone becomes occluded. The steepening barometric gradients associated with this development necessitate a lowering of the pressure at the center of the cyclone. However, the mechanism through which the removal of air from the region above a cyclone is achieved is by no means thoroughly understood and has never been satisfactorily explained. The problem is seen to be especially difficult when one considers that the surface winds which circulate around the center of a cyclone tend to blow inwards, a fact which apparently ought to counteract any further lowering of the pressure.

Weather phenomena associated with extratropical cyclones.— The first warning of the approach of a typical frontal cyclone in the Northern Hemisphere, such as is pictured in figure 123, is given by the barometer, which, if it previously had been rising or steady, will begin to fall. At about the same time a veil of high clouds of the cirrus type will be observed approaching from some westerly direction. Gradually these become more dense, eventually darkening the sky and obscuring the sun. Soon continuous rain (or snow) commences to fall, and the barometer drops with increasing rapidity. Let it now be assumed that the cyclonic system is traveling due east and the observer is situated at the latitude indicated by the dashed line I in figure 123. He will there experience, while the cyclone is still to the west of him, a wind that blows with increasing strength from some southerly direction. The continuous rain which is occurring falls from 'warm sector' air that has been raised off the earth's surface and is now flowing eastward aloft. When the 'warm front'— i.e., that portion of the boundary between the warm and cold air masses which constituted the forward side of the original wave-like disturbance—reaches the observer, the rate of fall of the barometer abruptly decreases, and a quick,

149

though not necessarily pronounced, veer of the wind to a more westerly direction occurs. At this juncture the nature of the weather also changes. The continuous rain ceases, and in its place a very fine drizzle accompanied by poor visibility (sometimes by fog) characteristically sets in. The drizzle falls from an unbroken layer of low-lying stratus clouds. The temperature of the air will have risen a few degrees, indicating the transfer of the observer from the cold, polar-type air into the warmer air of more tropical origin. Drizzle and poor visibility are typical of a warm sector over the ocean in middle and high latitudes.

While the observer is situated in the warm sector he will note that the barometer either remains steady, or continues to drop (if the cyclone is increasing in intensity), although in the latter case the rate of fall will be less than it was prior to the passage of the warm front. With the arrival of the boundary line marking the forward edge of the advancing cold air in the rear of the cyclone, an abrupt veer of the wind to a more westerly and northerly direction takes place. The passage of this line, which is termed the 'cold front,' is characteristically manifested by the occurrence of squalls and heavy showers (in fact moderate to heavy rain may start falling some time before the arrival of the wind-shift line). The barometer now commences to rise, the temperature falls, and the visibility improves. Subsequently a partial clearing of the sky occurs, although scattered showers continue, as a rule, for some time after the passage of the cold front and may never cease completely, even after the arrival of the anticyclonic system which normally follows the cyclone.

If the observer is situated at the latitude indicated by the dashed line II in figure 123 he will experience a sequence of events similar to those noted by an observer at the latitude of line I, except that the weather phenomena of the warm sector are absent and there takes place the passage of one front only, the 'occluded' front. The southerly wind in advance of it veers quickly to a westerly direction and the continuous prefrontal rain is replaced directly by the showery type of weather that characterizes the cold air in the rear portion of the cyclone.

If the observer is situated at the latitude of the dashed line III the center of low pressure will travel to the south of him and no front passage with sudden veering of the wind will be experienced. Instead the wind, which may originally have set in from a southerly or easterly direction gradually backs through north to northwest. The barometer exhibits no abrupt or discontinuous change in its rate of fall but rather a relatively gradual transition from falling to rising. The character of the weather also undergoes a comparatively slow change from precipitation of a continuous type to a showery type as the wind backs to the northwest.

The general sequences of weather phenomena described in the preceding paragraphs apply to the typical extratropical cyclone of the winter season in middle and high latitudes of the Northern Hemisphere. Naturally each individual storm differs somewhat in form from the model depicted in figure 123. However, there is one feature that is common to the structure of all young extratropical cyclones. It is an absence of symmetry and the presence of lines of discontinuity, in other words, fronts. On this account changes in the wind and in the state of the weather do not take place progressively over an extended interval of time but with a suddenness which is often surprising. Thus, a gentle westerly wind may be replaced by a northerly gale within the space of

APPENDIX

a few minutes.

Once an extratropical cyclone has become entirely occluded it has attained the last stage of its life history. It is then said to be an old cyclone. It assumes an almost symmetrical structure and the frontal system associated with it gradually dissolves. No longer do we find several distinct systems of clouds and precipitation which were characteristic of the partly occluded cyclone. The weather throughout the area surrounding the center becomes essentially uniform and tends towards the pure shower type.

Tropical cyclonic storms.—Tropical cyclones, in contrast to extratropical cyclones do not occur frequently. They form only over certain well-defined and limited water areas of the Tropics and quickly lose energy on reaching a large land surface. They also lose energy, although more slowly, as they progress toward middle latitudes over the oceans, usually at the same time expanding in size. On nearing or reaching the higher latitudes of the ocean a cyclone of tropical origin either dissipates or takes on the characteristics of an extratropical storm.

Tropical cyclones are confined most to six fairly distinct regions of great or small extend, four in the Norther Hemisphere and two in the Southern. These regions are (1) the entire West Indian region, including the Caribbean Sea, the Gulf of Mexico, and the waters east of Florida, in addition to much of the ocean east of the Antilles; (2) the southeastern North Pacific, known as the Mexican west coast region; (3) the Far East, which includes the entire area west of the Marianas and the Caroline Islands, across the Philippines and the China Sea, and northwestward to China and Japan; (4) the Arabian Sea and the Bay of Bengal; (5) a great stretch of ocean in the vicinity of and to the east of Madagascar, including the Mauritius and other islands; (6) the general region embracing Australian waters and eastward, including the archipelagoes to or beyond mid-Pacific.

The occurrence of tropical cyclones in the different months and for the six general regions is shown in the following table.

Occurrence of tropical cyclones of the six regions

	Jan.	Feb.	Mar.	Apr.	May	June	July	Aug.	Sept.	Oct.	Nov.	Dec.	Annual average number	Length of record (years)
Region I: North Atlantic Ocean	0	0	0	0	4	24	25	71	112	91	23	2	7	50
Region II: Southeastern North Pacific Ocean	0	0	0	0	3	17	17	25	50	26	2	1	5	27
Region III: North Pacific Ocean (Far East)	15	8	11	13	26	36	109	151	129	117	59	37	20	36
Region IV: Arabian Sea	x	x	x	x	5	11	3	0	2	10	8	2	2	23
Bay of Bengal	x	x	x	x	21	42	65	55	70	51	37	17	10	36
Region V: South Indian Ocean	113	115	98	68	25	3	x	x	x	7	33	58	7	70
Region VI: Australian waters to 160° E. longitude	54	49	58	29	7	7	x	x	x	4	10	22	3	84
South Pacific Ocean east of 160° E. longitude	69	47	64	18	2	2	x	x	x	4	8	31	2	105

x, Rare.

The number of tropical cyclones varies greatly from year to year. This irregularity in annual frequency is shown for three of the six regions of occurrence in the following tables. The greatest irregularity is shown for the North Atlantic, where the annual occurrence as indicated by the specific 10 years

151

(1927-1936) itemized in the table, ranged between 2, in 1929 and 1930, and 21, in 1933. Data for the 50-year period 1887-1936, summarized in the table, are from the records of the United States Weather Bureau. The table of eastern North Pacific tropical cyclones, covering the 27-year period 1910-1936, and is compiled largely from the records of the Zi-Ka-wei Observatory, Shanghai, China, the Weather Bureau, Manila, P.I., and the Central Meteorological Observatory, Kobe, Japan.

Occurrence of North Atlantic tropical cyclones, 1887–1936

	1887-1926	1927	1928	1929	1930	1931	1932	1933	1934	1935	1936	Total
May	1	0	0	0	0	0	1	1	1	0	0	4
June	17	0	0	1	0	1	0	1	1	0	3	24
July	18	0	0	0	0	1	0	3	1	0	2	25
August	46	1	2	0	1	1	3	7	2	2	6	71
September	85	3	3	1	1	3	3	5	2	1	5	112
October	74	2	1	0	0	1	3	4	3	2	1	91
November	19	1	0	0	0	1	1	0	1	0	0	23
December	2	0	0	0	0	0	0	0	0	0	0	2
Total	262	7	6	2	2	8	11	21	11	5	17	352

Average annual number, 7.

Occurrence of tropical cyclones of Eastern North Pacific, 1910–1936

	1910-1926	1927	1928	1929	1930	1931	1932	1933	1934	1935	1936	Total
May	0	0	1	1	0	0	0	1	0	0	0	3
June	7	2	2	1	1	0	1	1	0	0	2	17
July	11	2	1	0	0	1	0	1	1	0	0	17
August	12	1	1	2	1	1	2	1	0	2	2	25
September	32	3	3	3	0	4	1	0	1	0	3	50
October	17	1	2	0	3	0	0	0	1	0	2	26
November	2	0	0	0	0	0	0	0	0	0	0	2
December	1	0	0	0	0	0	0	0	0	0	0	1
Total	82	9	10	7	5	6	4	4	3	2	9	141

Average annual number, 5.

Occurrence of typhoons of the North Pacific, 1901–1936

	1901-1926	1927	1928	1929	1930	1931	1932	1933	1934	1935	1936	Total
January	13	0	0	0	0	1	0	0	0	0	1	15
February	7	0	0	0	0	0	0	0	1	0	0	8
March	7	1	0	0	1	0	1	0	1	0	0	11
April	10	0	0	0	1	0	1	0	0	1	0	13
May	21	1	1	1	1	0	0	0	0	0	1	26
June	31	1	0	3	0	0	0	1	0	0	0	36
July	79	2	4	5	5	0	2	4	1	2	5	109
August	121	4	3	2	2	5	3	1	4	3	3	151
September	93	4	3	7	1	4	1	4	6	4	2	129
October	78	5	3	5	1	4	3	4	6	4	4	117
November	40	2	2	2	1	3	1	2	2	1	3	59
December	27	0	0	0	0	1	1	0	4	3	1	37
Total	527	20	16	25	13	18	13	16	25	18	20	711

Average annual number, 20.

Many tropical cyclones originate in the more or less definite region known as the 'doldrums,' that narrow belt lying between the northeast and southeast trade winds. It is a region characterized by sultry air and calms or light and baffling breezes, interrupted by frequent rains, thunderstorms, and squalls.

The South Atlantic Ocean is free from cyclones of tropical origin, the reason being that the Atlantic doldrums are almost entirely north of the equator, their southernmost position, which occurs in March, being commonly between latitude 3 degree N. and the equator. They rarely reach south of that latitude and, if so, only for a brief period.

The origin of tropical cyclones is obscure in some of the details but the absence of such storms from the continental regions of the Tropics and their early disintegration after passing from the sea to the land go to show that their maintenance is dependent on a supply of water vapor which in the doldrums is present in the atmosphere in large amounts. The vapor-laden and heated air of these regions is underrun and forced upward by adjacent denser air—denser because drier and cooler. Thus is begin the process which later results in a continuing system of winds blowing around a moving center and constituting a tropical cyclone.

The developing storm drifts slowly westward with the current of free air and with this current it deviates more and more away from the equator after arriving at the western margin of the adjacent semipermanent 'high.' Here the winds turn poleward, as before explained, and this fact is reflected in the tracks of tropical cyclones, the centers of which commonly follow the free-air currents of the general circulation.

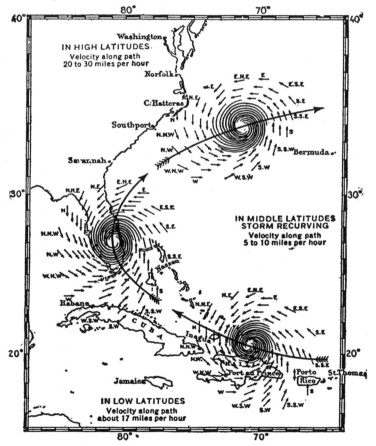

FIGURE 124.—Characteristic track and wind system of tropical cyclone of Northern Hemisphere.

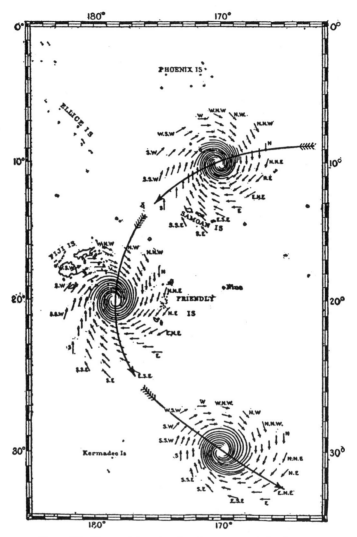

FIGURE 125.—Characteristic track and wind system of tropical cyclone of
Southern Hemisphere.

Fully developed, the tropical cyclone consists of a well-defined area, more or less circular in shape, throughout which the atmospheric pressure diminishes rapidly on all sides toward the center or point of lowest barometer, the rate of this diminution amounting in the case of severe storms to 0.01 or even 0.02 of an inch for each mile of approach. Within this area of barometric depression the winds blow with great force, the velocity of the moving air increasing with the steepness of the barometric slope or gradient, the direction, however, as previously explained being not toward but around the center. At the center itself—the point of lowest pressure—is a region seldom more than 10 or 20 miles in diameter throughout which calm or light air prevails.

APPENDIX

Here, too, the dense canopy of cloud which overhangs the storm area is pierced, forming the so-called 'eye of the storm.' The seas within this area are violent and confused, sweeping in from all sides with overwhelming violence. The gale winds, high seas, and torrents of rain which usually accompany tropical cyclones often cause great damage to coastal regions and to shipping in the path of the storm.

The size of tropical cyclones varies greatly. In the case of West Indian hurricanes, considering the area in which winds of gale force prevail, the average diameter is some 300 miles. The diameter of the area of destructive winds is, however, much smaller. The size of the vortex, or calm area, likewise varies. It rarely exceeds 15 to 20 miles in diameter and may be as little as 7 miles.

The usual track of the tropical cyclone resembles a parabola, of which the first branch of ten has its extremity in the region of the doldrums, as already explained, and the second branch, running to the east and north, has its extremity in middle latitudes. Here the storm either dissipates or takes on the form of an extra-tropical cyclone.

Figure 124 illustrates the typical parabolic track of a tropical cyclone of the Northern Hemisphere, with its attendant system of winds blowing counterclockwise and directed somewhat toward the center. The angle between the wind direction and the isobars seems to vary in the different quadrants. In several West Indian hurricanes that have been studied this angle was found to be greatest in the right hand rear quadrant, and least in the left-hand front quadrant. The statement is frequently met with that in cyclones of the South Indian Ocean the northeasterly and easterly winds (understood to mean before the storm recurves) seldom, if ever, blow around the center but almost directly toward it. These winds correspond in part to those of the right-hand rear quadrant of tropical cyclones of the Northern Hemisphere, in which quadrant as just stated, the inclination toward the center was also found to be greatest.

It will be noted from figure 124 that in portions of both right-hand quadrants the winds blow in the general direction of the line of advance of the storm. It is these violent, sustained winds, sometimes blowing in one direction for several days, that cause the storm waves and swells so destructive on the coasts visited by tropical storms. Careful observations made by use of tide gauges on the coast of the Gulf of Mexico show that the highest storm tide occurs in front of tropical storms and immediately to the right of the line of advance of the center.

In the Southern Hemisphere the winds blow in a clockwise direction about the center of a cyclone. Here again, the average trace of a tropical cyclone, arising in the region of doldrums, leads westerly at first. Its constantly increasing poleward component, however, carries it southwest, then south, and it finally recurves toward a southeasterly direction. In figure 125 is shown a characteristic track and wind system of a tropical cyclone in the Southern Hemisphere.

Although the average tracks of tropical cyclones in either hemisphere, arising in the doldrums, lead westward and poleward in a parabolic curve until in middle latitudes they recurve eastward, many individual cyclones deviate widely from the average. In the Northern Hemisphere, and possibly in the Southern also, the general direction of the first part of the track varies in different parts of the cyclone season, as does also the latitude of the vertex, or point where the trace recurves to the eastward. In the case of West Indian hurricanes the average direction of the first branch in the early part of the season, June and July is about 315 degrees. The direction of the first branch of August hurricane track is about 281 degrees.

With the advance of the season the direction of the first branch of the track inclines more and more to the northward and the latitude of recurve moves southward. The result is that the storms of September have generally recurved and started on the second branch of the track. Those which originated well out in the Atlantic have for the most part recurved near or to the east of the Bahama Islands, and the second branch has been about equal in length to the first. On the other hand, those which formed in the Caribbean Sea have generally recurved in the Gulf of Mexico and dissipated soon afterwards over the southern United States. In the case of October and November hurricanes the first part of the track had a 338 degree direction and the recurve was effected at still lower latitudes. Practically all storms of the period recurved and generally the second branch of the track was longer than the first. In these months, also, the presence of large anticyclones to the northward sometimes forces the tropical cyclone from a normal track, in extreme cases even causing it to move in such a way as to form a loop in its track. A

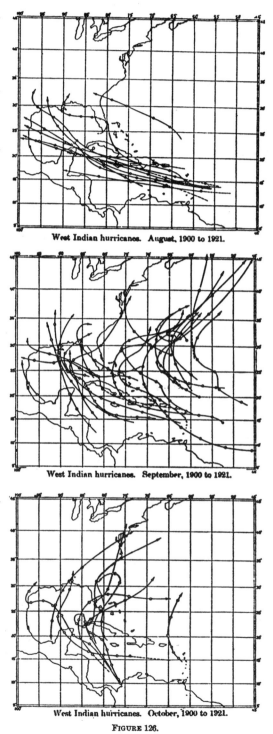

West Indian hurricanes. August, 1900 to 1921.

West Indian hurricanes. September, 1900 to 1921.

West Indian hurricanes. October, 1900 to 1921.

FIGURE 126.

156

study of the charts in figure 126 will reveal the characteristics of West Indian hurricane tracks just discussed. In figure 127 typhoons of the North Pacific have been classified according to average tracks. The percent frequency of each class and the period of the year during which typhoons are likely to follow that track are given in the table before the figure.

Early indications of tropical cyclones.—As will be explained later the modern development of radio weather reports at sea has made it possible for organized weather services to locate tropical cyclones when they develop and to issue warnings to shipping as to their size and probable movement. Although this advance has made it unnecessary for each ship to depend entirely upon its own observations and knowledge to avoid damage from the storm, it is still desirable that the rules for establishing the existence of a tropical cyclone and for locating its center be discussed.

These conditions are frequently accompanied by an unsteady barometer sometimes a little higher than usual.

During the season of tropical storms any interruption in the regularity of the diurnal oscillation of the barometer characteristic of low latitudes should be considered an indication of a change of weather. The barometer is by no means an infallible guide as a warning much in advance, but after the beginning of a storm it will more or less accurately indicate the rapidity of approach and distance from the center. Its indications should not be disregarded.

A long swell evidently not caused by the winds blowing at the place of observation is another warning that should never be overlooked. Frequently a swell from the direction of the storm sets in before any other indication becomes marked. Such a swell has in some instances given warning of a tropical cyclone days in advance of its arrival.

As the cyclone comes nearer the sky becomes overcast and remains so, at first with a delicate cirrus haze, which shows no disposition to clear away at sunset, but which later becomes gradually more and more dense until the dark mass of the true hurricane cloud appears upon the horizon. From the main body of this cloud portions are detached from time to time and drift across the sky, their progress marked by squalls of rain and wind of increasing force. Rain, indeed, forms one of the most prominent features of the storm. In the outer portions it is fine and mistlike, with occasional showers, these later increasing in frequency and in copiousness. In the neighborhood of the center it falls in torrents. The rain area extends farther in advance of the storm than in the rear.

Surrounding the actual storm area is a territory of large extent throughout which the barometer reads a tenth of an inch or more below the average, the pressure diminishing toward the central area, but with no such rapidity as is noted within that area itself. Throughout the outer ring unsettled weather prevails. The sky is ordinarily covered with a light haze, which increases in density as the center of the storm approaches. Showers are frequent. Throughout the northern semicircle of this area (in the Northern Hemisphere) the wind rises to force 6 or 8—the 'reinforced trades'—and is accompanied by squalls; throughout the other semicircle unsettled winds, generally from a southeasterly direction, prevail. Usually after the appearance of cirrus clouds, sometimes before, the barometer shows an unmistakable although gradual decrease in pressure. As the clouds grow thicker and lower and the wind increases the fall of the barometer usually becomes more rapid. When this stage is reached one may confidently expect a storm, and observations to determine the location of its center and its direction of movement should be begun.

The average tracks of the different classes of typhoons are the result of a study of 244 of these storms which occurred during the period 1884–1897, and are taken from the report of the director of the Hongkong Observatory for 1897. The relative frequency of each class and the period during which it is apt to occur are given in the following table.

Class	Frequency	Period
	Percent	
I$a\alpha$	10	Middle of June to end of September.
I$a\beta$	12	Middle of July to middle of October.
Ib	0	Late in the year.
Ic	4	June to the end of September.
Id	2	May to September, inclusive.
IIa	2	July, August, and September.
IIb	7	August and September.
IIc	3	June to September. Maximum in July.
IId	4	July and August.
IIIa	1½	October and November.
IIIb	1	October.
IIIc	4	July, August, and September.
IIId	15	June to October. Most frequent in August and September.
IIIe	12½	May to December.
IV$a\alpha$	8½	May to December. Rare in August.
IV$a\beta$	3	Beginning and end of typhoon season.
IVb	4½	September 1 to December 1. Most common in November.
IVc	4	Beginning and end of typhoon season. Most frequent in May.
IVd	1	April and December.

The appearance of the clouds and their value as warnings of tropical cyclones is described as follows by Faura in Cyclones of the Far East, by Jose Algué, of the Manila Observatory:

Long before the least sign of bad weather is noticeable and in many cases when the barometer is still very high—being under the influence of a center of high pressure, which generally precedes a tempest—these small isolated clouds (cirri, little clouds of a very fine structure and clear opal color resembling elongated feathers) appear in the upper regions of the atmosphere. They seem to be piled up on the blue vault of heaven and drawn out in the direction of some point on the horizon toward which they converge. The first to present themselves are few in number but well defined and of the most delicate structure, appearing like filaments bound together but whose visibility is lost before they reach the point of radiation. We often had an opportunity to watch them at the observatory of Manila, when the center was still 600 miles distant. The best times for observing the cirri are sunrise and sunset. If the sun is in the east and very near the horizon, the first clouds which are tinged by the solar rays are the cirro-strati which precede the cyclone, and they are also the last to disappear at sunset, inasmuch as they overspread the horizon. Such times are the best for determining the radian point of the cloud streaks and at the same time for ascertaining the direction in which the center lies. Later on the delicacy of form, which characterizes this class of clouds in its earliest stages, is lost, and the clouds appear in more confused and tangled forms, like streamers of feather work, with central nuclei, which still maintain this direction, so that the point of radiation can still be detected. In order to ascertain approximately the direction in which the center is advancing in its movement of translation, it is necessary to determine the changes of the radiant point at equal inter-

APPENDIX

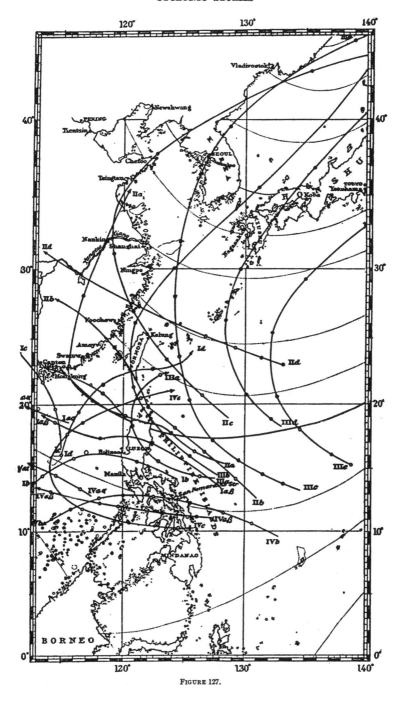

FIGURE 127.

159

vals of time and to compare them with the movements of the barometer. If the point of convergence does not perceptibly change its position, but remains fixed and immovable for a long time, even for several consecutive days, it is almost certain that the tempest will break over the position of the observer. In this case the barometer begins to fall shortly after the first cirrus clouds have been observed and sometimes even before. At first it falls slowly, without completely losing the diurnal and nocturnal oscillatory movements, but changing somewhat the hours of maximum and minimum. The daily reading is observed to be each day less than that of the preceding day. That part of the horizon in the direction of the storm begins to be covered by a cirrus veil, which increases slowly until it forms an almost homogeneous covering of the sky. This veil is known by the name 'cirro-pallium' of Poày, and is that which causes the solar and lunar halos, which are never absent when a storm approaches. Beneath the veil a few isolated clouds, commonly called 'cotton,' appear. They are much more numerous and larger on the side lying toward the storm, where they soon appear as a compact mass. At such times the sunrises and sunsets are characterized by the high red tint which the clouds assume, resembling a great fire, especially in the direction of the cyclone. The wind remains fixed at one point, showing only a few variations, which are due principally to the squalls, which continually exert their force within the limits of the storm. The low, or 'cotton,' clouds successively and from time to time cover the sky, throwing out occasional squalls of rain and wind; but, the squalls having passed, a lull ensues, the cirrus veil remaining, and likewise the hurricane bank of clouds, which seems fixed to the same spot in the direction of the storm. This state of the atmosphere continues until the bank of clouds invades the point of observation, in which case the squalls will be continuous and the wind will increase in violence each moment.

Fixing the bearing of the storm center.—It is very important to determine as early as possible the location and direction of travel of the center. While this can not be done with absolute accuracy with one set of observations, a sufficiently close approximation can be arrived at to enable the vessel to maneuver to the best advantage.

Since the wind circulates counterclockwise in the Northern Hemisphere, the rule in that hemisphere is to face the wind, and the storm center will be on the right hand. If the wind traveled in exact circles, the center would be eight points to the right when looking directly into the wind. We have seen, however, that the wind follows more or less a spiral path inward, which brings the center from 8 to 12 points (90° to 135°) to the right of the direction of the wind. The number of points to the right may vary during the same storm, and as the wind usually shifts in squalls its direction should not be taken during a squall. Ten points (112°) to the right (left in south latitude) when facing the wind is a good average allowance to make if in front of the storm, but a larger allowance should be made when in the rear. If very near the center the allowance should be reduced to 8 or 9 points (90° to 101°) in the front quadrants.

Based on the average, the following rules will enable an observer to fix approximately the bearing of the storm center.

In the **Northern Hemisphere,** stand with the face to the wind; the center of the cyclone will bear approximately 10 points to the observer's right.

In the **Southern Hemisphere,** stand with the face to the wind; the center of the cyclone will bear approximately ten points (112°) to the observer's left.

It may be noted here that the storm center almost always bears very close to 8 points (90°) from the direction of movement of the lower clouds of the cyclone. Therefore, when the direction of movement of the lower clouds can be observed it may serve as a more accurate indication of the bearing of the center than does the direction of the surface wind.

Further assistance in locating the approximate position of the storm center may be obtained in some instances by observations of the clouds. When the sky first becomes overcast with the characteristic veil of cirrus the storm center will most probably lie in the direction of the greatest density of the cloud. Later when the hurricane cloud appears over the horizon it will be densest at the storm center. The hurricane cloud, sometimes called the 'bar of the cyclone,' is a dense mass of rain cloud formed about the center of the storm, given the appearance of a huge bank of black clouds resting upon the horizon. It may retain its form unchanged for hours. It is usually most conspicuous about sunrise or sunset. When it is possible to observe this cloud the changes in its position at intervals of a few hours will enable the observer to determine the direction of movement of the storm.

Although the approximate bearing of the storm center is a comparatively easy matter to determine, and the direction in which the center is moving may be estimated with fair accuracy from the charted paths of similar storms (see figs. 126 and 127) it is by no means an easy matter for the observer to estimate his distance from the storm center. The following old table from Piddington's 'Horn Book' may serve as a guide, but it can only give an imperfect estimate of the distance and too much reliance must not be placed upon it.

Average fall of barometer per hour	Distance in miles from center
From 0.02 to 0.06 inch	From 250 to 150.
From .06 to .08 inch	From 150 to 100.
From .08 to .12 inch	From 100 to 80.
From .12 to .15 inch	From 80 to 50.

This table assumes that the vessel is hove-to in front of the storm and that the latter is advancing directly toward it.

With storms of varying area and different intensities the lines of equal barometric pressure (isobars) must lie much closer together in some cases than in others, so that it is possible only to guess at the distance of the center by the height of the mercury or its rate of fall.

A further source of error arises because storms travel at varying rates of progression. In the Tropics this ranges from 5 to 20 miles per hour, generally decreasing as the storm track turns poleward and recurves, increasing again as it reaches higher latitudes. In the North Atlantic its rate of progression may amount to as much as 50 miles per hour. Within the Tropics the storm area is usually small, the region of violent winds seldom extending more than 150 miles from the center. The unsettled state of the barometer described heretofore is usually found in the area between 500 and 1,000 miles in advance of the center. This gives place at a distance of 300 or 400 miles to a slow and steady fall of the mercurial column. When the region of violent winds extending about 150 miles from the center is reached, the barometer falls rapidly as the center of the storm comes on, this decrease within the violent area sometimes amounting to 2 inches.

Because of this very steep barometric gradient the winds blow with greater violence and are more symmetrically disposed around the center of a tropical cyclone than is the case with the less intense cyclones of higher latitudes. After a tropical cyclone has recurved it gradually widens out and becomes less severe, and its velocity of translation increases as its rotational energy grows more moderate. Its center is no longer a well-defined area of small size marked by a patch of clear sky and near which the winds blow with the greatest violence. Out of the Tropics the strongest winds are often found at some distance from the center.

Handling the vessel within the storm area.—If, from the weather indications given above and such others as his experience has taught him, the navigator is led to believe that a tropical cyclone is approaching, he should at once—

First. Determine the bearing of the center.

Second. Estimate its distance.

Third. Plot its apparent path.

The first two of the above determinations will locate the approximate position of the center, which should be marked on the chart. The relation between the position of the ship and the position and prospective track of the center will indicate the proper course to pursue (a) to enable the vessel to keep out of an escape from the dangerous semicircle and to avoid the center of the storm; (b) to enable the vessel to ride out the storm in safety if unable to escape from it.

Should the ship be to the westward of the storm center before the path has recurved, it may be assumed that the latter will draw nearer more or less directly. It then becomes of the utmost importance to determine its path and so learn whether the vessel is in the right or left semicircle of the storm area.

The right and left semicircles lie on the right and left hands, respectively, of an observer standing on the storm track and facing in the direction the center is moving. Prior to recurving, the winds in that semicircle of the storm which is more remote from the equator (the right-hand semicircle in the Northern Hemisphere, the left-hand semicircle in the Southern) are liable to be more severe than those of the opposite semicircle. A vessel hove-to in the semicircle adjacent to the equator has also the advantage of immunity from becoming involved in the actual center itself, inasmuch as there is a distinct tendency of the storm to move away from the equator and to recurve. For these reasons the more remote semicircle (the right hand in the Northern Hemisphere, the left hand in the Southern Hemisphere) has been called the dangerous, while that semicircle adjacent to the equator (the left hand in the Northern Hemisphere, the right hand in the Southern Hemisphere) is call the navigable.

In order to determine the path of the storm and consequently in which semicircle the ship finds herself, it is necessary to wait until the wind shifts. When this occurs, plot a new position of the center 10 points (112°) to the right of the new direction of the wind as before, and the line joining these two positions will be the probable path of the storm. If the ship has not been stationary during the time between the two sets of observations (as will indeed never be the case unless at anchor), allowance must be made for the course and distance traveled in the interim.

162

APPENDIX

Two bearings of the center with an interval between of from 2 to 3 hours will, in general, be sufficient to determine the course of the storm, provided an accurate account is kept of the ship's way, but if the storm be moving slowly a longer interval will be necessary.

Should the wind not shift, but continue to blow steadily with increasing force, and with a falling barometer, it may be assumed that the vessel is on or near the storm track. Owing to the slow advance of storms in the Tropics, a vessel might come within the disturbed area through overtaking the center. In such a case a slight decrease in speed would probably be all that would be necessary, but it should be born in mind that the storm path is by no means constant either in speed or direction, and that it is particularly liable to recurve away from the equator.

A vessel hove-to in advance of a tropical cyclonic storm will experience a long heavy swell, a falling barometer with torrents of rain, and winds of steadily increasing force. The shifts of wind will depend upon the position of the vessel with respect to the track followed by the storm center. Immediately upon the track, the wind will hold steady in direction until the passage of the central calm, the 'eye of the storm,' after which the gale will renew itself, but from a direction opposite to that which it previously had. To the right of the track, or in the right-hand semicircle of the storm the wind, as the center advances and passes the vessel, will constantly shift to the right, the rate at which the successive shifts follow each other increasing with the proximity to the center; in this semicircle, then, in order that the wind shall draw aft with each shift, and the vessel not be taken aback, a sailing vessel must be hove-to on the starboard tack; similarly, in the left-hand semicircle, the wind will constantly shift to the left, and here a sailing vessel must be hove-to on the port tack so as not to be taken aback. These two rules hold alike for both hemispheres and for cyclonic storms in all latitudes.

It must not be forgotten that the shifts of wind will only occur in the above order when the vessel is stationary. When the course and speed are such as to maintain a constant relative bearing between the ship and storm center, there will be no shift of wind. Should the vessel be outrunning the storm, the wind will indeed shift in the opposite direction to that given, and a navigator in the right semicircle, for instance, judging only by the shifts of wind without taking into account his own run, might imagine himself on the opposite side. In such a case the barometer must be the guide. If it falls, one is approaching the center; if it rises, one is receding.

An examination of figure 128 shows how this is. A vessel hove to at the position marked b, and being passed by the storm center, will occupy successive positions in regard to the center from b to b4, and will experience shifts of wind, as shown by the arrows, from East through South to SW. On the other hand, if the storm center be stationary or moving slowly and a vessel be overtaking it along the line from b4 to b, the wind will back from SW. to East, and is likely to convey an entirely wrong impression as the location and movement of the center.

Hence it is recommended that a vessel suspecting the approach or proximity of a cyclonic storm should stop (if a sailing ship heave to on the starboard tack) for a while until the path of the center is located by observing the shifts of the wind and the behavior of the barometer.

If the wind remains steady in direction and increases in force in heavy squalls while the barometer falls rapidly, say, at a greater rate than 0.03 of an inch per hour, the vessel is probably on or near the track of the storm and in advance of the center.

In this position, with plenty of sea room, the proper course is to run with the wind well on the starboard quarter, if north of the equator, and on the port quarter if south. The vessel will thus be in the navigable semicircle and be constantly increasing her distance from the center. The wind will draw more forward as she recedes from the center, but the compass course first set should be adhered to until well clear.

The procedure is the same if the observations place the ship anywhere within the navigable semicircle.

The most critical situation is that of a vessel finding herself on the forward quadrant of the dangerous semicircle, particularly if at some distance from the center, where the wind shifts but slowly and the barometer indications are undecided, both causes combining to render the bearing of the center uncertain.

The general object, however, of putting as much distance as possible between the ship and the storm center should be kept in view.

With steamers this may not be difficult, although, should the storm be

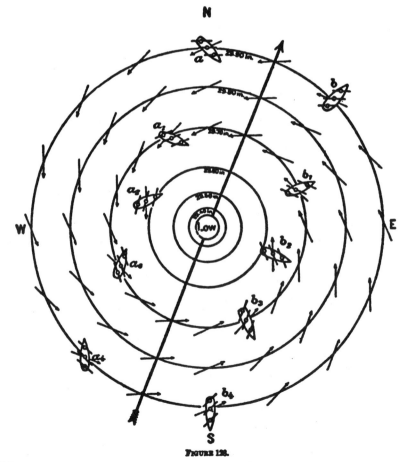

FIGURE 128.

APPENDIX

recurving, the course first set may have to be subsequently altered in order to continue to draw away.

A sailing vessel will be set by the wind directly toward the path of the storm and may become involved with the center without being able to avoid it. If so caught in the dangerous semicircle, a sailing vessel should haul by the wind on the starboard tack when in north latitude (on the port tack in south latitude), keep coming up as the wind draws aft, and carry sail as long as the weather permits. If obliged to heave to, do so on the starboard tack in north latitude and on the port tack in south latitude.

This maneuver, while it may not carry a vessel clear of the storm track, will make the best of a bad situation.

A vessel so hove to will find the shifts of wind drawing aft, enabling her to come up to them instead of being headed off, as would be the case on the other tack.

Moreover, since the sea changes its direction less rapidly than the wind, the vessel will come up more nearly head on to the old sea, instead of having it more abeam as on the opposite tack.

A general rule for sailing vessels is always to heave to on whichever tack permits the shifts of wind to draw aft.

Figure 128, representing a cyclonic storm in the Northern Hemisphere after recurving, illustrates graphically these rules for sailing vessels.

For simplicity the area of low barometer is made perfectly circular and the center is assumed to be ten points (112°) to the right of the direction of the wind at all points within the disturbed area. Let us assume that the center is advancing about NNE. (22°), in the direction of the long arrow, shown in heavy full line. The ship *a* has the wind at ENE. (67°); she is to the left of the track, or technically in the navigable semicircle. The ship *b* has the wind at ESE. (112°) and is in the dangerous semicircle. As the storm advances these ships, if lying to, *a* upon the port tack, *b* upon the starboard tack, as shown, take with regard to the storm center the successive positions *a1, a2,* etc., *b1, b2,* etc., the wind of ship *a* shifting to the left, of ship *b* to the right, or in both cases drawing aft, and thus diminishing the probability of either ship being struck aback, with possible serious damage to spars and rigging, a danger to which a vessel lying to on the opposite tack (i.e., the starboard tack in the left-hand semicircle or the port tack in the right-hand semicircle) is constantly exposed, the wind in the latter case tending constantly to draw forward. This ship *b* is continually beaten by wind and sea toward the storm track. The ship *a* is drifted away from the track and should she be able to carry sail would soon find better weather by running off to the westward.

Should steamers find it necessary to heave to the method of doing so must depend upon the position within the storm area.

A steamer is concerned more with the damage resulting from heavy seas than from wind; furthermore a steamer is not dependent for the course upon the direction of the wind, but is free to maneuver to keep away from the storm center, where the heaviest and most confused seas are found, unless other circumstances, such as proximity to the land, prevent.

If unable to escape from the storm, and this can be done only in low latitudes when the storm covers a comparatively limited area, the principal object of a steamer is to avoid the center of the storm.

Referring to figure 128, it is obvious that in the Northern Hemisphere if a steamer finding herself in the left-hand (navigable) semicircle at *a* or *a-1* should obey the rule for sailing vessels and heave to on the port tack, her head will lie *toward* the storm track and the greatest danger. On the other hand, under the same circumstances, if the steamer heaves to on the starboard tack, her head will lie *away* from the storm track and such headway as is made will all be in the direction of safety.

Following the same reasoning, a steamer in the Northern Hemisphere caught in the right-hand (dangerous) semicircle at *b, b-1* (fig. 128) and obliged to heave to should do so head to sea, because in this case both the wind and sea are constantly beating her toward the storm track, and when lying to, head to sea, less leeway will be made than in any other position.

Many steamers behave better when hove to with the sea astern, or on the quarter, but the adoption of this method must depend upon the position of the vessel within the storm area. Referring again to figure 128, it will be clearly seen that, in the Northern Hemisphere, if in the forward quadrant of the left-hand semicircle at positions *a, a-1,* a steamer may safely heave to with the sea astern or on the starboard quarter. This course, however, should never be attempted when in the forward quadrant of the right-hand semicircle (positions *b, b-1*) for the reason that any headway made would be, in all probability, toward the storm center where the high and confused seas would be likely to inflict damage.

If, in spite of all endeavors, the storm center should pass directly over a vessel she will experience a short period of calm, but the seas will be high, confused, and dangerous, being swept in from all directions. After a short interval the wind will burst with hurricane force from a point directly opposite to that from which it was blowing before, and the vessel must be prepared to meet it and to avoid being caught aback.

Maneuvering rules.—The rules for maneuvering, so far as they may be generalized are:

NORTHERN HEMISPHERE

Right or dangerous semicircle.—Steamers: Bring the wind on the starboard bow, make as much way as possible, and if obliged to heave to, do so head to sea. Sailing vessels: Keep close-hauled on the starboard tack, make as much way as possible, and if obliged to heave-to, do so on the starboard tack.

Left or navigable semicircle.—Steam and sailing vessels: Bring the wind on the starboard quarter, note the course and hold it. If obliged to heave to, steamers may do so stern to sea; sailing vessels on the port tack.

On the storm track, in front of center.—Steam and sailing vessels: Bring the wind two points (22°) on the starboard quarter, note the course and hold it, and run for the left semicircle, and when in that semicircle maneuver as above.

On the storm track, in rear of center.—Avoid the center by the best practicable route, having due regard to the tendency of cyclones to recurve to the northward and eastward.

SOUTHERN HEMISPHERE

Left or dangerous semicircle.—Steamers: Bring the wind on the

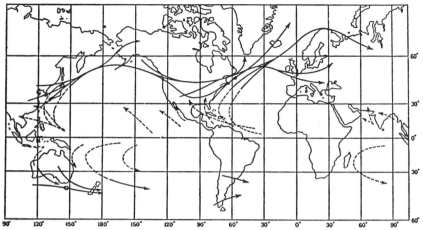

FIGURE 129.—Best known storm tracks of world. (Dotted lines, tropical cyclones; solid lines, extra-tropical cyclones.)

port bow, make as much way as possible, and if obliged to heave to do so head to sea. Sailing vessels: Keep close-hauled on the port tack, make as much way as possible, and if obliged to heave to do so on the port tack.

Right or navigable semicircle.—Steam and sailing vessels: Bring the wind on the port quarter, note the course and hold it. If obliged to heave to, steamers may do so stern to sea; sailing vessels on the starboard tack.

On the storm track, in front of center.—Steam and sailing vessels: Bring the wind two points (22°) on the port quarter, note the course and hold it and run for the right semicircle, and when in that semicircle maneuver as above.

On the storm track, in rear of center.—Avoid the center by the best practicable route, having due regard to the tendency of cyclones to recurve to the southward and eastward.

The above rules depend, of course, upon having sea room. In case land interferes, a vessel should heave to, as recommended for the semicircle in which she finds herself.

Bibliography

Bowditch, Nathaniel, *American Practical Navigator*, U.S. Navy Hydrographic Office, H.O. Publication No. 9, 1958 edition

Bullen, Frank, *A Sack of Shavings*, London, Collins

Coles, K. Adlard, *Heavy Weather Sailing*, 4th Edition, Revised by Peter Bruce, International Marine Publishing, 1992, USA. UK—Adlard Coles Nautical, An Imprint of A&C Black

Cunliffe, Tom, *Heavy Weather Cruising*, International Marine Publishing, 1988. UK—Fernhurst Books.

Farrington, Tony, *Rescue in the Pacific*, International Marine, 1995. UK—Published as *Rogue Storm*, Waterline Books, An Imprint of Airlife Publishing Ltd.

Henderson, Richard, *Sea-Sense*, International Marine, 1983. UK—Waterline Books, An Imprint of Airlife Publishing Ltd.

Hinz, Earl, *Understanding Sea Anchors and Drogues*, Cornell Maritime Press, 1992

Hiscock, Eric, *Cruising Under Sail, Incorporating Voyaging Under Sail*, Adlard Coles Nautical, 1981

Howard, James D., *Handbook of Offshore Cruising*, Sheridan House Inc., 1994. UK—Adlard Coles Nautical, An Imprint of A&C Black

Howard-Williams, Jeremy, *Sails*, 6th Edition, Adlard Coles Nautical, An Imprint of A&C Black, 1988

James, Robert A., *Ocean Sailing*, Nautical Publishing Co. Ltd., 1980

Jordan, Donald J. and Carol L. Hervey, *Drogue Design to Prevent Breaking Wave Capsize*, U.S.C.G. Research and Design Center, 1988

Kemp, Peter, Editor, *The Oxford Companion to Ships and the Sea*, Oxford University Press, 1979

The New Glenans Sailing Manual, Staff of Glenans Sea Center France, pub. Sail Books, 1978. UK—David & Charles, Pub. Ltd.

BIBLIOGRAPHY

Shane, Victor, *Drag Device Data Base,* 3rd Edition, Para-Anchors International

Street, Donald M., Jr., *The Ocean Sailing Yacht,* W.W. Norton, 1973. UK—Imray, Laurie, Norie and Wilson

Taberly, Eric, *Practical Yacht Handling,* David Mc. Kay Co., 1980

Voss, J.C., *Venturesome Voyages of Captain Voss;* originally pub. in 1900, reprinted and available through The Maritime Museum of British Columbia, 28 Bastion Square, Victoria B.C. V9W 1H9 Canada (604-385-4222)

Para-Anchor Suppliers

AUSTRALIA
P. Lublin Associates PTY Limited, 10 King Street, Balmain, NSW 2041; tel./fax (02) 810-5568

Para-Anchors Australia, 18 Gippsland Highway, Sale, Victoria 3850,; tel. 61-51-444-333

GERMANY
Blue Water GMBH, Speditionstr. 17, 40221, Dusseldorf; tel. 0211 39 10 69, fax 0211 9 30 49 43

ICELAND
Valdimar Samuelson, Kleifaras 3, 110 Reykjavik; tel. 354 587 2524, fax 354 587 2526

NEW ZEALAND
Safety at Sea (AUSTALIASIA) Ltd., Gaunt Street, Westhaven (P.O. Box 91107), Auckland; tel. (09) 309-9111, fax (09) 309-92-11

W.A. Coppins, 255 High Street, Motueka; tel./fax 64-3-52-87296

USA
Gerrard Fioentina Marine Sales, 311 22nd Street, San Pedro, CA; tel. 800-835-5601, fax 310-831-9000

Para-Anchors International, P.O. Box 19 Summerland, CA 93067; tel. 805-966-0782, fax 805-965-1935

Para-Tech Engineering Co., 6702 Hwy. 82, #3, Glenwood Springs, CO 81601; tel. 970-928-9356, fax 970-928-9237

Shewmon, Inc., 1000 Harbor Lake Drive, Safety Harbor, FL 33572; tel. 813-447-0091

West Marine, P.O. Box 50050, Watsonville, CA 95077-5050; tel. 800-538-0775

UNITED KINGDOM
Cruising Home Limited, 12 Westfield, Highnam, Gloucestershire, GL2 8LX; tel./fax (0) 1452-503705

Glossary

Drogue—any device that slows a boat's progress through the water to improve steering control and give it directional stability. Can be tires, various kinds of warps, gale rides, series drogues. Sometimes a small cone-type sea anchor is used as a drogue, to gain steering control

Heave-to—a verb, described throughout this handbook

Hove-to—past tense; after you heave-to you are lying hove-to

Pennant lead—the line used to alter the lead of the main sea anchor rode, it is similar to a barber-haul

Sea anchor—a device designed to stop a vessle's forward progression through the water, and to stabilize its attitude to the wind. Normally streamed off the bow. Can be a para-anchor, large personnel chute, small cone made of canvas, with a metal hoop mouth and a hole at the tip of the cone

Slick—the turbulent wake created when a boat's keel stals and createsd vortices, which disturb the water pattern on the windward side of the boat; sometimes called a smooth

For readers who use metric measurements we offer the following guidelines:

Lineal inches x 25.3999 = millimeters
Lineal feet x 0.3048 = meters
Lineal fathoms x 1.8288 = meters

Square feet x 0.0929 = square meters,
   therefore 100 square feet of sail area would be
   equivalent to 9.29 square meters of sail area

Fractions of inches to millimeters
$1/4$" = 6.35 mm
$5/16$" = 7.94 mm
$3/8$" = 9.53 mm
$7/16$" = 11.11 mm
$1/2$" = 12.7 mm
$9/16$" = 14.29 mm
$5/8$" = 15.88 mm
$3/4$" = 19.05 mm
$7/8$" = 22.22 mm
1" = 25.4 mm

Index

Page references in *italics* indicate diagrams or photographs. References followed by *n* indicate footnotes.

INDEX

INDEX

About the Authors

Lin and Larry Pardey have voyaged together for over 26 years, covering the equivalent of 5¹/₂ circumnavigations on board their own self-built cutters, *Seraffyn* and *Taleisin*. Larry worked as first mate on a 140-ton, 85-foot schooner, *Double Eagle*, voyaging from Newport Beach, California, to Hawaii and back and along the Mexican coast before meeting Lin. He, along with Leslie Dyball, won the handicap prize for first overall in the exceptionally stormy 1974 Round Britain two-handed race. Lin and Larry have delivered two dozen boats across oceans and raced their own and others' boats. Their interest in storm tactics has led them to research both older and modern methods of heaving-to, by talking and corresponding with sailors from dozens of countries, by working with Victor Shane at the Drag Device Data Base, and by testing both on their own boat in hurricane-force winds and on modern boats off the Cape of Storms, in South Africa.

Larry was selected as the 1996 winner of the International Oceanic Award, given by the Royal Insitute of Navigation under the sponsorship of the Little Ship Club of London and presented by Her Royal Highness, the Princess Royal, Princess Anne, for the most meritorious voyage of over 2,000 miles using traditional methods of navigation. Larry's award was for 30 years of successful voyaging, covering more than 150,000 miles on 21 different vessels and using only sextant and chronometer, including his 2,840-mile voyage in 1995 from Fernando do Noronha to Horta, in the Azores.

In March 1996 Lin was presented with the Ocean Cruising

ABOUT THE AUTHORS

Club Award for the person who has "done the most to foster and encourage ocean cruising in small craft and the practice of seamanship and navigation in all branches," at the Royal Thames Yacht Club, in London.

Articles by Lin and Larry have appeared in *Sail* Magazine, *Cruising World, Woodenboat* (USA), *Practical Boat Owner, Yachting Monthly, Classic Boat* Magazine (UK), *Cruising Helmsman* (Australia), *South African Yachting,* and *Nautica* (Brazil).

Their nine books have been published in both the United States and England; two have been translated into German and Japanese. Lin and Larry are currently writing a new book, *The Cost-Conscious Cruiser.* Their most recent voyage took them to Scotland and Norway, and *Taleisin* is ready for another voyage, either west or north in the spring of 1998.

What do you mean, "Just turn and run before it"?

Notes

Other information-packed books by Lin and Larry Pardey

The Cost Conscious Cruiser -
Champagne Cruising on a Beer Budget
Publication date November 1998

Twenty-five chapters to help you get out cruising affordably, confidently and enjoyably. Sections on planning your escape, finding that affordable second-hand boat or building your own, cost-effective outfitting, getting good value from your cruising funds, how to control the emotional costs once you get out cruising. Each chapter will give you food for thought and guidelines that have worked for hundreds of voyagers. Two special sections give ideas for hands-on upgrades you can do yourself, and answers to ten questions most frequently asked by potential cruisers.

Hardbound, 320 pages, 100 illustrations, $29.95 - ISBN 0-9646036-5-9

The Self Sufficient Sailor - revised edition

A distillation of what the Pardey's have learned in 150,000 miles of sailing on their own and scores of other boats they have delivered and raced. How to sail in comfort and safety on a pay-as-you-go plan including - earning your way, hitch-hiking across the oceans, freeing the galley slave, inspecting and maintaining your rigging, plus many other fact-filled chapters. This best-selling book has been widely recommended by well-known sailors ranging from Donald M. Street, author, sailor and raconteur, Bernard Moitessier, sailor, writer and adventurer and owner of Joshua, Tom Linskey, now Senior Editor at Sail Magazine, and Danny Greene, sailor and Editor with Cruising World Magazine.

Hardbound, 317 pages, illustrated, $29.95 - ISBN 0-9646036-7-5

$\rightarrow$

The Capable Cruiser

From Priorities for Choosing a Cruising Boat, to maintenance at sea, to taking care of yourself and your crew and the seamanship that ensure a safe voyage, this book is a logical companion to the Self Sufficient Sailor, the Cost Conscious Cruiser and Storm Tactics Handbook. The Pardeys analyse how and why 29 cruising boats were lost in one popular anchorage, plus 20 other aspects of open-water voyaging. Of special interest to many would-be cruisers is their discussion of how to write and sell cruising stories.

Hardbound, 400 pages, illustrated, $32.00 - ISBN 0-9646036-2-4

The Care and Feeding of Sailing Crew - second edition

Useful, up-to-date information on all facets of preparing for blue-water adventure or a cruise along your local shoreline, from outfitting a galley to cooking in rough weather, to scheduling and planning meals with individual health needs taken into account. Special chapters include handling seasickness, managing cash and currency while you cruise, designing efficient refrigeration and water tank systems. A daily account of the problems of caring for the crew during a 49 day, 4,500 mile voyage across the storm-tossed waters between Japan and Western Canada, including the recipes that were used, precedes each chapter. All in all this makes a highly readable, information-packed volume.

Hardbound, 388 pages, illustrated, $35.00 - ISBN 0-9646036-0-8

Look for these and other Pardey Books at your favorite bookseller or order direct by calling 1-800-736-4509 in the USA (1-707-822-9063 from outside the US) or 01743-235651 in the UK.